The American Journalists

JOURNAL IN JAIL

Thomas Low Nichols

ARNO
&
The New York Times

Collection Created and Selected
by Charles Gregg of Gregg Press

Reprint edition 1970 by Arno Press Inc.

LC# 71-125709
ISBN 0-405-01690-5

The American Journalists
ISBN for complete set: 0-405-01650-6

Reprinted from a copy in
The New York Public Library

Manufactured in the United States of America

JOURNAL IN JAIL,

KEPT DURING A

FOUR MONTHS' IMPRISONMENT

FOR LIBEL,

IN THE JAIL OF ERIE COUNTY,

BY THOMAS L. NICHOLS.

BUFFALO:
A. DINSMORE.

1840

Entered, according to Act of Congress, in the year 1840, by THOMAS L. NICHOLS, in the Clerk's Office of the District Court of the Northern District of the State of New York.

PREFACE.

I shall expend no eloquent asseverations in trying to persuade the reader of my "Journal in Jail," that it was not written for publication; the internal evidence being sufficiently conclusive.

The only manner in which "my *too partial friends* prevailed upon me to give it to the world," was by plausibly representing that thereby I might "turn an honest penny."

Those who wish to know any thing more about the book, are respectfully referred to the Table of Contents.

CONTENTS.

INTRODUCTION.—Arrival in Buffalo: Starting the Buffalonian: case of Rathbun: finding endictments: the conspiracy. P. 9, 12.

THE TRIAL.—Judge Stryker: evidence: Hiram Pratt charged with felony: Rathbun Allen: charge, verdict and sentence.
13, 18.

JOURNAL.—JUNE 18. Egotism: reception: sensations: my cell: first night in prison: epigram. - - - - 19, 23.

JUNE 19. The prison at morning: diet: presents: toast: philosophy: Prison Pindarics. - - - - 23, 27.

" 20 Checkered life: surveillance and censorship: malice of the clique: indignation: letter to the sheriff. 27, 31.

" 22 Dreams and memories of home: slanders: character of woman: originality: my first kiss in prison. 31, 35.

" 23 Lake steamboats: pious meditations: christian fiends: Hiram Pratt's religion: the assignees: Prison Pindarics—"I saw the Devil in a dream." - 36, 41.

" 24 "'Tis woman's kindness:" reasons for rhyming: letter from Miranda: reply. - - - - 41, 47.

" 25 A visiter: flowers and verses: curious philosophical experiment: W. L. Mackenzie: Job's comforter: what I love: magic: Biddle: Benton. - - 48, 54.

" 26 One week in prison: changing places: more severity: the Mayor: epigram on a banker. - - 54, 58.

CONTENTS.

JUNE 27 Epigrams; letter; lines to Miranda; boy editor; experience; history. - - - - Page 59, 65.
" 28 Rathbun; moral influence of the clique; little girls; to Mackenzie in prison. - - - - 66, 69.
" 29 Fourth of July; letters of Junius. - - 70, 73.
" 30 SUNDAY. Piety in prison; letter; running for office; Songs of Solomon. - - - - - - 74, 76.

JULY 1. James Gordon Bennett; imitation; Canadian prisoners. 76, 79.
" 2 Letter from Julia; magic; moral reform; married ladies' *billet doux.* - - - - - - 80, 82.
" 3 Maledictions; poor debtors; Bill Smith; music, lice and poetry. - - - - - - 83, 89.
" 4 The celebration; bedbugs; patriotism. - 89, 93.
" 5 Monotony; philosophy of happiness; who need pity; character of Buffalo; boys and girls; jealousy. 93, 97.
" 6 Letter to Rosalie; Richelieu, Bulwer. - 97, 101.
" 7 Frank Johnson; upstropulousness; a Fourth of July incident; patriotism and poetry. - - 101, 104.
" 8 Music; prison correspondence. - - 104, 109.
" 9 Industry; friendship of Hiram Pratt. - - 110.
" 10 Trials; prison letters; public meeting at Hamburgh. 111, 114.
" 11 Grand juries; more endictments; letter to Mr. G.; a clergyman sent to State Prison; letter to the sheriff. 114, 119.
" 12 Reduced to jail fare; John Wentworth; roses. 119.
" 13 Depression; stimulants; prison fare. - 120, 122.
" 14 Bigamy; romance in jail; letter to Miranda. 122, 126.
" 15 "Yes, all the bright summer is passing away." 127.
" 16 Letter from Rosalie; reply; sunset. - 127, 131.
" 17 Smuggling; letter from Julia; angels' visits. 131, 135.

CONTENTS.

JULY 19 Good things, Henry Clay, letter from Mackenzie, album poetry. - - - - Page 135, 139
" 20 Suicide, a visit, sensibility. - - - 140, 141
" 21 Solomon, Samson, Science Jack; - - 141, 145
" 25 Popularity, Rosalie, hot times, tortures, Rathbun in jail, to Rosalie, to Miranda, auto-biography. 145, 158
" 31 Appleby, letter from sister. - - - 158, 161

AUGUST 3. Poetry and things. - - - - 161, 162
" 6 Hell and mint juleps. - - - 162, 163
" 7 Letter to Rosalie, to Mrs. —— - 163, 167
" 10 Prison amusements, public feeling. - 167, 168
" 12 Newspaper writings. - - - 169, 171
" 13 John Low, honesty. - - - 171, 172
" 16 Women, kissing, poetry. - - - 172, 175
" 17 Big licks, mint juleps, Platonism. - 175, 177
" 18 Serenades, riots. - - - - 178
" 20 The sailor in jail. - - - 179, 182
" 21 The pillow of love, companions. - 182, 186
" 22 Morals, injustice of women. - - 186, 191
" 28 Letter to Rosalie. - - - 194
" 30 Letter to Julia, album verses. - - 198, 201
" 31 A ghost story. - - - - 201, 203

SEPT. 1. Pelham's heroines, letter to Rosalie. - 203, 206
" 5 New novels. - - - - 207, 209
" 6 Extravagance and egotism. - - 209, 211
" 7 Poetry, to Edward. - - - 212, 215
" 11 Letter from Solomon Southwick. - 216, 220
" 12 Scene in the Recorder's court, lines to the Hon. H. J. S. 220, 222
" 13 Sentiment, an angel, crazy woman. - 223

CONTENTS.

SEPT. 17 Observations, retrospections and recollections, a Recorder and a Judge. - - Page 223, 227
" 18 Temperance, bustles. - - - 227
" 22 Texas, hermaphrodite. - - 228
" 24 Cards, Heacock's pamphlet, Alice and Rosalie. 229, 231
" 29 Ambition, pleasure, power, pious advice. - 232
OCTOBER 2. Kidnapping, Song of the imprisoned. 233, 235
" 4 Authorship, suffering. - - - 235, 237
" 10 The benefit, address, people's verdict. - 238, 240
" 15 Secrets of the cellar, - - - 241, 244
APPENDIX. - - - - - 245, 248

INTRODUCTION.

I came to Buffalo in the autumn of 1837. Neither when I left New York, nor when I arrived here, had I any intention of staying. I wished to see Niagara. Once here, one of those unaccountable impulses seized me, which neither Phrenology nor Animal Magnetism can explain, but which have always seemed to me like the palpable power of Destiny, and I decided to wander no farther.

I wrote for the Buffalo Commercial Advertiser, and sent the patriot news to Bennett's Herald. The former establishment paid me five dollars a week; the latter, three dollars a day for not one third the matter I wrote for the former. One day a printer came to me—"We are going to get up a little paper," said he, "just for the fun of it, and we want you to write some little things for it." I went to their room. They had got an old fount of type, and had a paper, two wide columns on a page, partly set up. I scribbled a paragraph or two; and on Christmas morning appeared the first number of the BUFFALONIAN.

New Year's saw the second, of which I furnished nearly all the matter; and such was its success, that we began to think of making it a permanent establishment. It was printed tri-weekly—then daily—enlarged and re-enlarged, until it began to assume respectable dimensions. The first number contained an inquiry in relation to the proceedings of the assignees of B. Rathbun. The matter was followed up. I became acquainted with the facts of the case, and found that a clique of sharpers had entered into a deliberate and treacherous conspiracy to crush him, and divide among themselves an estate of over two and a half millions; and they have done it.

I visited Rathbun in prison. I was struck with his noble appearance, and his calm endurance of a confinement I then thought intolerable, though I have since endured a worse, in the same gloomy, miserable cell that then confined him. He had lain there for twenty months. When I wrote the account of that visit, and described his situation, tears wet the paper on which I wrote, and they glistened on many a manly cheek when it was read. I insisted he should have bail; his friends were incited to exertion, and he soon walked our streets, and on every side met kind greetings, except from those whose ingratitude and treachery made them ashamed to look him in the face.

I did not hesitate to publish the facts which came to my knowledge respecting the assignees and the persecutors of Rathbun. The public knew them to be true; and three successive attempts to get me endicted for libel failed. A fourth, by some means, was successful; and a grand jury found two indictments: one for libels on Hiram Pratt and others, which has never been tried; and the other for a libel on H. J. Stow, on which I was convicted and imprisoned. The Pratt endictment was for calling him a rascal and a purjurer, and the only case in which the public took any interest. That of Stow was always considered of trifling consequence. He was a lawyer and a bank attorney; and in the libellous paragraph was charged with being the tool of his employers, and compromising the honor of his client by inducing him unnecessarily to turn State's evidence, against his relation and benefactor. But more of that on the Trial.

I attended the trial of Rathbun at Batavia, and saw such a mockery of justice as I had never dreamed could be carried on in an American court. It filled every honest bosom with indignation. And all around were his fiendish persecutors. I have never doubted that there were strong reasons for the partiality of the judge; and still less, that the jury—but three of whom belonged to the regular panel—were packed, perjured, and paid. The world knows the result. Time passed. I did not cease to denounce the conduct of Hiram Pratt and the "Clique" who had conspired to destroy Rathbun, defraud his creditors, and enrich themselves; nor did they cease to persecute me, and use every mean and despicable measure to stop my paper. In the spring of 1839, they formed a conspiracy to kidnap me one night, take me out of town, and tar and feather me, and at the same time demolish my printing materials. A gang of ruffians was got together, bribed, and disguised. By a most singular chance, I escaped the party lying in wait for me. The office was thoroughly demolished; but the paper did not stop, and other measures were resorted to.

THE TRIAL

It was at the June term of the General Sessions. The Hon. James Stryker, First Judge of the county, Indian Agent, &c.; a man notorious for his debauched habits and pecuniary unscrupulousness, and who has since been endicted by a grand jury of this county for felony, presided at the trial. For several terms previous, he had been absent, and now came from Washington on purpose to preside at this term. It has been asserted that funds were furnished by certain persons here, to pay his board and get him here; and it has also been said, that in case matters went as desired, accommodations were to be granted, to save his household furniture from being sold under the sheriff's hammer. This was asserted, at the time, without denial.

The libel case came on, before a crowded court room: H. W. Rodgers, District Attorney, and Mr. Skinner, a distinguished lawyer from Genesee county, engaged especially for this trial, for the People; and T. T. Sherwood, Esq., one of the most able and distinguished lawyers in Western New York, for the Defendant. A strong effort was made to get on the trial of the Pratt endictment, for which we had made the fullest preparations, and in which all felt so much interest, but without avail. He dared not come to trial; and the Stow case was called, and a jury empanelled.

On the part of the people it was proved, that at the time of the publication charged as libellous, I was editor of the paper, and a partner in the proprietorship. They also proved, that I was absent at the time the article was published, forty miles distant, and had been, a number of days previous, and the paper under the control of another; nor did they make it appear that I knew, or could have known, of its publication: and on this, my counsel moved the court to instruct the jury to bring a verdict of not guilty; but the court held that though absent, and ignorant of the matter published, my name being in the head of the paper as editor, was enough to convict me of a malicious libel!

On the part of the defence it was proved, that Stow was, at the time, the attorney of the Bank of Buffalo, of which Hiram Pratt and Orlando Allen were officers; and that he had also been their private attorney: that a chancery bill had been drawn by Stephen G. Austin, in behalf of himself and other stockholders, charging Pratt, as President of the Bank of Buffalo, with many crimes and misdemeanors, *some of which amounted to* FELONY; which bill was produced, and my counsel offered to read it and *prove the charges true*, but the court would not permit it! It was then proved, that to settle this bill, prevent its being filed in chancery, and smother investigation, Pratt paid from 7,500 to 10,000 dollars; and that H. J. Stow actively assisted in carrying out this *arrangement*.

It was also proved that Stow was the counsel of Rathbun Allen, nephew of B. Rathbun; and that he had often said that he could not be convicted on any of the endictments pending against him. It was shown how Allen was arrested in New Orleans, and kept for several months in the jail of that city, in the hot season; then brought round to New York by sea, *in irons*; brought to Buffalo, thrown into jail, and there kept so closely that no friend was allowed to see him—none but Stow and the District Attorney, and such persons as they chose to bring to him; where the state prison was held out to him on one hand, and on the other, liberty and all the enjoyments of life—and the terms, but to give such evidence as they wanted to convict his uncle at Batavia. Such means might have produced the required effect upon a stronger mind and firmer principles than those of Rathbun Allen. He was taken to Batavia, closely guarded until he had given the required evidence, when he was restored to perfect freedom.

The Court, during the whole trial, ruled out offered evidence; and exceptions were taken to many of its decisions. The trial commenced on Friday morning: the arguments of counsel closed Saturday evening; when Judge Stryker delivered to the jury, one of the most extraordinary charges ever heard in any court in Christendom—to almost every proposition of which, my counsel took exceptions. The jury went out late in the evening, and at about midnight, came in and said they could not agree. At this time, it is said they stood, four for convicting, and eight for acquitting. The Court *charged them over* again, insisting still more strongly upon my guilt, and its own unheard-of construction of the law; and they went back, and at about one o'clock on *Sunday morning*, brought in a verdict of GUILTY.

Some of this jury were for convicting me before the trial. Of the rest, some were ruled by the Court, and some agreed to a verdict to avoid sitting up all night, after the fatigue of a two weeks session! This is from their own subsequent declarations. The scene of the trial was in character with the whole proceedings. The house was thronged with my friends: around and within the bar, sat the clique of my persecutors, Pratt, Potter, Stow, &c. &c.; and the latter, except when on the stand, was generally at the elbow of the District Attorney! And such was their anxiety for the result, that several of them remained until the verdict was brought in; either waiting in the court, or watching the door of the jury room.

On Monday, a motion was made by my counsel, for a suspension of sentence while the case should be carried up to the Supreme Court, on a bill of exceptions. At the same time, my bail advised and requested me to avoid being sentenced, as I could expect no lenity. This I wholly refused. That I should run away, had been the hope and expectation of my enemies, from the time they found the endictments; and for two days after my conviction, I was at perfect liberty. On Tuesday morning, the motion for suspension of sentence was argued; and as in the case of Rathbun, refused. A plea was then made in mitigation, supported by an affidavit of the printer who set up the libellous paragraph, and swore not only that I was absent and had no control of the paper, but that the paragraph was not in my handwriting; but this plea was rudely interrupted, and I stood up to receive the sentence of the Court. After patiently listening to nearly a half hour's vituperative blackguardism, undignified and gratuitously insulting, I was sentenced to four months imprisonment in the jail of Erie county, and to pay a fine of one hundred and fifty dollars; to remain committed until paid.

JOURNAL IN JAIL.

BUFFALO JAIL, June 18, 1839.

I never, for any length of time, kept a Journal. Once, when out of employment, I kept one a few weeks; but the moment I was busy again, I threw it aside. I am not enough of an egotist! When young, I destroyed all I wrote, at intervals, because my scribblings came so far short of what I was conscious they ought to be; and of my favorite productions, and those most admired by my friends, I have no copies. But now, a journal will be resource, a pastime, a pleasure; and the reflections of a four months imprisonment—all the curious thoughts and incidents of so novel a situation, must not be lost; therefore, I'll keep a Journal.

It was about twelve o'clock, when an officer of the court escorted me from the court house to the jail—a very short walk, and one in which men are often given to trembling of the knee joints—but this is when they walk from the jail to the court house. I was received by the jailer in that singularly amiable and taking manner, with which a jailer always receives a prisoner, or an officer serves a bench warrant or capias, where there is no resistance. And now I am seated in the cell occupied so long by Benjamin Rathbun, No. 20; the farthest of the upper range, and the most secluded in the prison. It is a strange coincidence. His enemies have been mine: I am here for advocating his cause. I did it honestly and fearlessly. Shall I sleep the less soundly?

What are my sensations? I have no new ones. For months, I have made up my mind, in case of conviction, to this result. I have become accustomed to the idea—indeed, I have always thought that if I could be imprisoned a few months, without crime or disgrace, I would choose to experience a scene of life so new. So having made up my mind to it, there was no thrill of horror, no depression; nothing but my stern philosophy, which makes the best of every situation in life. What if I am in a convict's cell? Greater men than I—wiser, better men, have been in worse. John Bunyan, in prison, wrote the Pilgrim's Progress—a book which will live through all time, and all eternity, I suppose. In prison, Cervantes wrote Don Quixotte—an immortal work of genius, speaking after the manner of men in regard to the immortality, though in their style there is no inconsiderable similarity. Thus, some of the noblest efforts of the human mind have been made while the body was imprisoned; and it would appear that in "durance vile" there is something peculiarly favorable to mental exertion.

But had I ever so strong a disposition to have "sensations" and "emotions," I have been too busily engaged. First, there was my cell to see to. This interesting place is eight feet long, and about the same height, and nearly five feet in width—I am sure it is more than four—though I have nothing to measure with—but not much: as I look, and compare it with the length of my body, it seems to grow narrower. The walls are covered with a very dilapidated papering, put on when Lyman Rathbun was first confined in it. It has no window; and all the light comes through the iron door, constructed after the similitude of a checker board; whence it is said by the witty ones, of a man in jail, that he is playing checkers with his nose—an observation, of which I am in a situation to be often reminded. This light is never very powerful; and as it is obliged to first force its way through a narrow, grated window, six feet from the door aforesaid, by the time it gets through, it becomes exceedingly weak, and very much exhausted.

The *furniture* of the cell consisted, first, of a frame, on which was a piece of sacking, which may once have been stretched, but now, by numerous occupants, is sagged down most pitifully: this was intended to sleep upon. Next, two blankets, filthy to the last degree: then, a thing, which I was informed was a pillow; but never could have guessed for what purpose it was intended, as the blankets were clean in comparison: and lastly, a wooden pail: and this was all—and this, had I no money or friends, is all I should have!

"I suppose I can send for my trunk, and make my cell as comfortable as I like," said I to the jailer.

"Certainly. You can get what you please, for yourself."

Pretty soon came a friend, with a mattrass and bedding. Didn't the black blankets and the coal-pit looking pillow get marching orders? Then came my trunk, with books and stationery; which I had packed in readiness, *two days before.* Then came a carpenter, and made me shelves, a turn-up table, and a tiny wash stand. Then a chair, and other *et ceteras.* My friends came pouring in to see me, and I was in excellent spirits.

And now 'tis night. The lock is turned upon me;

and a babel of confused sounds, with the horrid music of clanking chains, has gradually sunk into silence. I have thought the matter over, and without one emotion of regret. Men were offering to bet, yesterday, that I would not be in court to-day, to receive my sentence. In the name of Heaven, do not people know me better than that? Forty thousand devils could not frighten me from one firm resolve, though each were as black as devils are painted, with horns, and hoofs, and tails: how much less, that diminutive imp, Hiram Pratt, and a paltry imprisonment!

> Low born and meanly bred; yet not content
> To be a *little* knave, as Heaven intended;
> On notoriety his soul is bent—
> It comes, with infamy and hatred blended!

I'll sleep on that.

In Jail, June 19, 1839.

I slept, and never in my life slept more soundly. I awoke as the gray light of morn was struggling through the gratings. As I lay upon my cot, I could see a few square feet of green grass, a branch of foliage, and a very little strip of beautiful blue sky. And now

I hear a wild free bird carolling its glad strain outside the window opposite my cell. He is twittering, but I hope he don't *twit;* nor rejoice to find that men, who make prisoners of so many of his little warbling tribe, sometimes get caged themselves; for it would be very unamiable and unchristian of him.

"You had better take care of your things, when you leave your cell," said the jailer.

"Why!" I exclaimed in astonishment; "you havn't any *thieves here* I hope! What will the world come to?"

One of my generous friends has ordered my food to be sent from Carr's Washington Coffee House, and excellent it is. No *man* could have arranged that server so tastefully: none but a woman would have the tact to send precisely what I wanted. So, in the matter of diet, I am very comfortably provided for. What my fellow prisoners live upon, has not yet entered into my investigations. There is what they call soup, for breakfast, and mush and molasses for supper. I can't find as they have any thing like dinner.

There are about fifty prisoners, making plenty of society, such as it is; nor is there any lack of conversation, which is of the character that might be expected from men confined for every grade of crime, from vagrancy to murder. The delicate and refined, whose ears have been unpolluted by vulgarity, can form no idea of it. How it would have shocked me once! and now, it seems, by far, the worst feature of the place.

My cell—thanks to the kindness and sympathy of my friends—is filled with presents. I have cake, wine, cigars—to give away, for I never use them—fruit, and flowers. Most of them are from ladies, and some brought by themselves. Mrs. W. H. Pierce, one of the most excellent women and best actresses on the American Stage, has sent me a bottle of delicious wine. I drink to her—May it always be her fortune to be surrounded by those who will appreciate her private worth and professional merits!

Another day has nearly past; nor have I found it impossible to be happy in a prison. The idea of being shut up, in a place of tomb-like aspect and dimensions; where all the glories and beauties of the external world are but in memory; where each wandering zephyr finds its difficult way through double grates of massive iron—and, ere it reaches you, becomes tainted with the foul stench of a prison—is not of the most delightful: yet there are many things far worse.

"What can be more terrible?" asked my friend—a sweet lady, who was shuddering with the apprehension.

"Many things, my dear," said I. "Disgrace, dishonor, the consciousness of a wilful wrong—any of these are worse than a mere imprisonment; especially, when produced by means so foul and disgraceful."

Such is my philosophy. Happiness dwells in the soul; and in those of noble natures, depends not upon circumstances. The prisoner in his cell may have more enjoyment than he who is surrounded by the trappings of wealth and the pageantry of power.

The sun is declining into the west. I have a little glimpse of the beauty of his evening drapery of clouds; but I cannot see his setting. That lone bird has come again to my window—is he sent? or is he the imbodiment of some fair spirit that still hovers about me? At all events, he is answerable for the production of these—

PRISON PINDARICS.

"That strain again!" Oh, joyous bird,
How blithely dost thou sing!
As if no breaking heart were near,
As if no bosom quaked with fear
Of punishment, by crime incurred—
And on thy buoyant wing,

Thou in an ever glorious sky,
　Didst fly around the world;
Nor ever dreamed of captive's sigh,
Nor knew that groans of misery
Rose from the stifled dungeon's air;
Nor dreamed, so near thee, black Despair
　His Demon flag unfurled!

Sing on, bright bird!
　With joy amid this gloom;
　E'en in this living tomb,
Thy song is heard.
One captive answers to thy lay,
　With heart as light as thine;
With voice as cheerful, blythe, and gay;
And as he sings "Dull care, away,"
　Still dazzling hopes around him shine,
And all the future gleams as bright
As diamonds in the flashing light.

Erie County Jail, June 20.

"Well, Nichols, yours is a checkered life," said my medicinal friend, C. C. Bristol, of "Compound Fluid Extract of Sarsaparilla" celebrity.

"Very much so, just now," said I, glancing at the door of my cell.

A change has come over the aspect of my affairs. The christian fiends—my meek and lowly persecutors—are not yet satisfied. They have taken away my wine and porter; but that I don't care for. It was against the law for them to allow it to come into my cell; but once here, they need not have taken it away.

All my friends, without distinction, are to-day ordered to be excluded—even my counsel find it difficult to see me. The door of my cell is kept fastened, and I am placed under the most rigid surveillance. The jailer has orders to examine every scrap of paper that I send out, *to see that there is nothing libellous.* Such are the orders! I am watched as if I were some ferocious beast, or terrible giant, and men were quaking in hourly fear that I should do them an injury.

This making the jailer a censor of the press, is one of the richest jokes yet; but perfectly in keeping with the whole conduct of the stupid clique, and the contemptible underlings, who execute their malicious designs, and are the instruments of their tyránny.

Will they take away my pen and paper?—will they dare? They even threaten to put me on the "ball and chain gang;" and with one leg chained to a heavy iron ball, drive me out to work upon the public roads! Why not? A disgraceful statute gives them the power; and nothing but fear, I know, prevents them from carrying it into effect. One would suppose that the imprisonment and fine, of such unexampled severity, would be sufficient. But nothing short of my complete ruin will satisfy the malice of those who are determined to destroy me. Talents, genius, character, friends, and the noblest and purest motives, all go for nothing, when the infamous *clique* has doomed a man to destruction. There is nothing noble, manly, generous, or honorable about them. Tyrants to those in their power, servile to those above them, they unite the meanness of petty knaves, to the malignity of those who hate all that is purer and better than themselves.

And what have I done, to provoke such rancorous hatred, and such deep revenge? Was I ever, in my life, guilty of one act of malignity? Did I ever do an intentional wrong, or refuse any reparation in my power, for an unintentional one? Never! And what has been my course in this city? Have I not consulted its best interests, and advocated them with energy, perseverance and effect? Has any good object appealed in vain to my sympathy, or lacked my assistance? Have I ever defended the strong, and oppressed the weak? And have I not received the approval of the virtuous and the good? Have I not had the delicious friendship and holy sympathy of woman's heart?

Have not the last whispered requests of dying innocence and loveliness been in my behalf?—and looks not that sweet angel from Heaven upon me in my lonely cell, at this midnight hour, her radiant smiles lighting up the gloom of the dungeon?

I wish to know *who* is the responsible agent in the treatment I am receiving, and have written the following letter

To the Sheriff of Erie County:

Sir,—After being treated, for two days, with lenity and kindness, I find myself suddenly deprived of what liberty the limits of the jail allowed me, and shut up in my cell, without any sufficient or apparent reason. My friends—even my legal advisers and attorneys, are denied admittance, it is said, but I am loth to believe it—by your orders.

Such a course is, I scarcely need say, perfectly unprecedented, under such circumstances, in this country; and I hope and believe, that the Sheriff of Erie county is *above* the *corrupt influences* which, for a time, seem to overpower all law and justice.

If these things are by your orders, I wish to know it; if not, I trust you will immediately give such, as will cause the laws to be executed, *without exceeding them.* Tyrannous oppression ought not to belong to your character; nor should unmanly subserviency to a vile and corrupt clique: but, Sir, if this course is continued, it will be very difficult to persuade the people of this county that *they do not.*

I have the honor to be, &c. &c.,
Your Prisoner,
THOS. L. NICHOLS.

Addressed,
CHARLES P. PERSON, Esq.

SATURDAY, JUNE 22, 1839.

I was awakened, this morning, with the clanking of chains and fetters, the dull springing of rusty padlocks, and the creaking of iron doors. Sweet dreams had blessed my pillow—dreams of home and its beloved inmates—dreams of the fresh air of my native hills, where I roved a free and happy boy, my eye kindling with rapture, as I stood upon the brow of the precipice, with a broad expanse of fertile fields and sparkling waters spread out before me; and my bosom swelling with the glorious enthusiasm that the works of God inspire in him to whom he has given a soul to feel their mighty and mysterious influences. No prison walls, nor bolts, nor bars, confined me then. The wild eagle that screamed among the crags, was not more free. Those days are passed. I was thrown upon the world, and left to battle with its untoward fortunes and high-handed villanies, with all my energies; and though I look back, with fond recollections, upon "days long vanished," my heart is never "filled with pain." There is no act of my existence—no deliberate act—that I regret: none but what, were the truth told, and my motives appreciated, every virtuous man would applaud. I am not free from human follies and foibles; but wrong and outrage can never stain my name; nor guilt, nor dishonor, blacken my character.

Now—the tongue of Slander is busy. Now I am in a prisoner's cell, all the mean, the malignant, the cowardly, will join together, to calumniate and abuse me. Will the noble, the generous, the fair, believe them? Will they see me wronged more foully, and abused more outrageously, than my worst foes have ever accused me of wronging others? No! I have seen the curl of the scornful lip, and the flashing of the indignant eye, when mean and cowardly malice has attacked a fame as pure as yonder spot of cloudless sky, that beams, like an opening in heaven, through the grates of my prison; and I shall not lack for defenders. But if I do, what matter? The world's praise or censure, its good or bad opinion, would never cause me to exult, in the one case, or give me a moment's disquietude in the other; for I am certain, that a sense of right has ever been with me a motive far higher and more active than the love of approbation, or the fear of censure.

But of all these stupid slanders, the most absurd is the one now most industriously circulated,—that I have been the calumniator of female virtue! As well might I try to quench the light of my existence, the sunshine of my prosperity, and the mildly beaming effulgence that throws a halo of hope over the darkest hour of despondency.

I have found man changeable, false, and treacherous; but woman, *never*. I have found man at once a tyrant and a slave, cringing to power, and oppressing weakness; but woman, never. I have found man selfish, malignant, cowardly, mean, and cruel; but never woman! I have had the friends of my prosperity, and those who flocked around me when the heavens were bright, desert me in the first hour of my misfortune, and fly from the first storm of persecution; but they belonged not to the angelic sex, to the disinterested, the faithful, and the true. Though man should desert me; though purse-proud Villany should stalk in triumph, and *Corruption* walk unblushingly in open day; though I were by all beside forgotten; Beauty's eye would fill with the tear of generous sympathy, and woman's smile would joyfully welcome me again to light and freedom.

They have brought me a bundle of books; so that now—between the resources of writing, reading, singing, eating and sleeping—I can pass the time happily, if I am kept in my cell ever so closely.

I never read, before, "The Humors of Eutopia;" but it has some very amusing passages—The comic ones are especially excellent. It would dramatize effectively—make a good comedy, or cut up into farces. This is a sort of thing I never did, and probably never shall do. There is little invention required—and 'tis well for some geniuses there is so little. There is not much in the world. Men imitate, modify, arrange: God creates; and he is most godlike who nearest approaches Him in this. I wonder if there be one original thought—one pure invention—in Shakspeare?

An incident, savoring of the romantic, occurred to me to-day. A *petit* and very pretty *brunette*, with beautiful black eyes, a rich color, and pouting lips, with a most enchanting "How d'ye do my dear?" expression, came to see me. My cell door

happened to be open, and she looked in upon its
arrangements. She knew me—as every body does—
but I had never seen her; and spoke so pityingly
of my imprisonment—said it was such a shame,
such an outrage, to treat me as they did; and spoke
so feelingly, that my arm stole gradually around
her—I drew her imperceptibly nearer—I looked in
her bright eyes, as I thanked her for her sympathy,
and assured her, that with her, I could be happy any
where—what in gallantry could I have said beside?—
our cheeks approached each other—then our lips,
and * * * Now what else could I have done?
After going so far, there was surely no retreating.
And a kiss—such a pure, chaste, Platonic kiss as
that, is as innocent as apple dumpling. Her husband
might have been jealous, had he seen us; but it
would have arisen entirely from a misapprehension.
Ladies have sent me beautiful *boquets* of fragrant
flowers, and delicious strawberries and cream, and
unnumbered luxuries—but this was my first kiss
in prison.

  Like a flower on the desert—a cot in the wild;
   Like a beacon, that guides the tossed sailor to rest,
  Was the dear face of woman, as on me she smiled—
   Were the lips, that in prison, I first to mine prest.

BUFFALO JAIL; SUNDAY, June 23, 1839.

Nature is smiling around me, as if it reflected the glories of the Almighty. Through the bars of my prison, I see glimpses of green grass, rich foliage, and the pure, holy sky; and then the chains clank, and the hinges creak, and the hoarse curse falls harshly on the ear.

How delightful would be a walk along the beach of yonder lake, the music of whose resounding shore, I almost fancy I can hear. I see the bright waves come dancing in the sunlight, eager to embrace the pebbly beach. I see the white sails of the distant vessel, and the lofty pipes of yonder proud steamer, as she walks the waters, dashing the spray before her, and leaving a long track of glittering foam behind. Magnificent creature! I hear the hard beating of thy restless heart—I see the struggle of thy massive limbs—I behold thee, matchless in beauty, moving over the blue waters, which are proud to bear thee on their bosom!

Hark! I hear the glad sound of the "church going bell." The people are gathering to the house of prayer. All worldly thoughts are banished, all worldly passions hushed to holy rest. Every heart is raised in prayer and praise to God—every eye looks up to the bright heavens, full of penitence, and humble faith. They enter the doors of the Sanctuary, consecrated to the worship of the Great Creator, and Father of all. All is hushed and silent. Now from the secret altar of each heart, holy aspirations are rising to the throne of the Eternal. Father in heaven! how beautiful is the worship of thy house! The voice of solemn prayer is heard, and the music of God's praise from many voices, attuned to divine harmonies. The holy word of inspiration is read, and all listen with that earnest devotion, that would lay up every word as a heavenly treasure in the heart. "Oh, God! One day in thy courts is better than a thousand."

There all is humble penitence, heavenly love, and holy rapture. The sweet spirit of christian charity broods over them—a light of more than mortal glory beams from every eye—a smile of more than mortal pleasure lights up every countenance. All sinful thoughts—all unholy desires—all mad and revengeful passions, and grasping avarice, and sinful pride, and worldly vanity—all are hushed. The heart is purified, warmed, melted, and man becomes almost an angel, in the presence of his merciful Creator. Such is religion—such are the influences of christianity. What a heavenly picture!

I would not write a sermon, but holy thoughts are clustering about me, and tender recollections clinging to my heart. In the prayers that go up daily from the altar of my home, I am sure, paternal love never forgets me. What must a mother, a sister, feel? Grieve not, beloved ones. I am not unhappy. Heaven smiles upon me, and a thousand kind and generous hearts surround me with an atmosphere of love. Four months—all the bright summer will pass away, and then I will be with you, unless the fiends in human shape, pursue me still.

"Fiends!"—I forget. Heaven pardon me! They are christians! They profess the holy religion of love and mercy. They "do unto others as they would that others should do unto them." They "*forgive* their enemies, and bless those who curse them, and pray for those who despitefully use, and persecute them." They are holy, humble christians—pillars of the church of God. So is, or rather *was*, the Judge who sentenced me—and the District Attorney too, he is one of the meek and lowly ones!

How pleasant it is to see christians like these! So full of love, and charity and forgiveness! Heaven must smile upon and bless them. Truly, they are the salt of the earth!—a city set on a hill that cannot be hid!—a light to the world! The grace of God burns in their hearts—peace and mercy attend them. They go about doing good. The widow and the fatherless bless them! *Verily*, they shall have their reward.

But really, now—the idea of Hiram Pratt being a christian would be most ludicrous, were not hypocrisy too solemn a subject for laughter. One being laughs every time he thinks of it. Satan, in the depths of his infernal abode laughs at the withering hypocrite. He is not alone. He is not the only one of this banditti, who has

"Stolen the livery of the court of Heaven
To serve the Devil in."

But he has had the hardihood to make himself the most conspicuous. He has thrust himself into the highest office in the city; and when his resignation, and those of his infamous parasites who elected him, were demanded by two thirds of the citizens of Buffalo, he and they refused to obey. A more consummate hypocrite, and a more false-hearted knave, walks not the footstool of God. Of the other assignees, Allen is a blustering, pompous blockhead; and Clary is supposed by many to be the soul of the conspiracy, the wire-puller of the clique, and the one who plots what the others execute. He cannot be guiltless—and is probably most guilty—but he keeps behind the curtain; the infamous work goes on, but his hand is not seen.

It is not the assignees alone who are engaged in this robbery. They were obliged to buy up others with a share of the spoils—or more likely, the conspiracy at first included a dozen, more or less. If such men lived in Italy or Spain, and had the requisite physical courage, they would form a banditti. If they were sailors, there is no doubt they would be pirates. Some of them used to be smugglers!

But of Satan's laughing. The idea has got into my head and twisted itself about until it has come out in the following—

PRISON PINDARICS.

I saw the Devil in a dream,
   A holding both his sides:
With laughter wild, I heard him scream,
And shake his tail, till it did seem,
   The whip of one who rides
     And makes it crack
     O'er horses' back,
As on his course he glides.

JOURNAL IN JAIL.

But what could make the Devil laugh?
  For laugh he did right well;
And never when their wine they quaff,
Did louder peals e'er shake the raf-
  Ters of the roof of hell!
And I wondered what the devil sent
This sudden burst of merriment.

"Look here!" said Satan—"ha! ha! ha!
  My conscience! what a whopper!
Just hear that 'pious rascal' lie."
"Which one, good Devil?" then said I—
"Which!" said the demon, "ha! ha! ha!
  Him with the CAMBLET WRAPPER!"

The cause was plain, I asked no more,
  But cut my stick and run;
And Satan laughed, and laughing swore,
  'Twas devil-ish good fun.

MONDAY, June 24, 1839.

'Tis woman's kindness—woman's cheering voice,
  Gladdens the prisoner in his gloomiest hour;
'Tis woman's pen, that bids me still rejoice,
  And nerves my soul to brave my tyrant's power.

Her friendship soothes me, and her warmest love
  Wakes sympathetic passion in my breast;
Nor will I ask if colder hearts approve,
  Nor wound a bosom that yearns to be caressed.

My thoughts gush out in rhymes, which, even by myself, I cannot consider very poetical; and which I would not write, only they come running through my head, and haunt, and haunt me, until (the only way to lay them) I put them on paper; and then they are forgotten. It is strange; but since my days of school-boy doggerel, I have not written so much of this sort of thing, as since I have been shut up closely in this horrid cell.

I was thinking of my charming friend, Miranda. I was reading her letter, breathing in every paragraph a strength of devoted attachment, none but a woman, and such a woman, can feel. She has a rare and noble heart; kind, generous, grateful, and full of sympathy and every gentle emotion: and yet, if I mistake not greatly, there is no lack of spirit; and those bright eyes would flash resentment, as warmly as they beam with enthusiasm—or love. But I shall copy and preserve my first letter in prison.

LETTER FROM MIRANDA.

"My Dear Friend:—It is with mingled emotions of anger, sorrow, and disappointment, that I lift my pen to address you. I am angry with those base villains who have been the cause of your confinement in that horrible place; I am deeply sorry for your misfortunes; and I am disappointed in the first and strongest wish of my heart, which is for your society. I did not really think they would be so cruel, so basely inhuman, as to confine you, until I saw your next morning's paper, and learned from that, that it was too true; that there are men allowed to live, and breathe the pure air of heaven, who are so destitute of principle or humanity, as to send a man to prison for speaking the truth. I had hoped that those fears we felt, were groundless, and that you would be spared to liberty and your friends; but hope was vain. Suspense is ended, and you are—O God! must I say it?—locked up in that dreadful place—and I, my only relief from the anguish I feel, am writing to you.

"What a change a few days has wrought! I am very unhappy — very lonely. Every body — every thing—seems to wear a look of gloom and disappointment. To me, all looks dull and cheerless. All has changed. I walk about, but at every turn I seem to meet with a new disappointment. It was so last night. I went to the window and threw it open; and although it was a calm and beautiful evening, I felt more disappointed than ever. I looked around, and felt as if I was searching for something I could not find.

"It is late now, and I am quite alone; but early in the evening a friend of yours called to see me. How delighted I was to see him! I thought my heart would burst with joy. And yet I dared not speak—dared not ask a single question. My suspense defies comparison. I wanted to hear how you were; I wanted to hear all about every thing; and yet, if you had seen me, you would have thought me the most indifferent person in the world. I dared not appear otherwise. I was afraid of betraying a single wish or thought. He told me he had been to see you in the afternoon. Oh! how I wanted to ask him a thousand questions in a moment; yet I asked but two, and those with as much indifference as if they were of no consequence. I asked him how you were, and if you did not dislike being in jail. Oh! kind Heaven only knows how much I wished to converse with him on that subject for one hour; but it was not to be, and he soon left me. I hope he will call again soon. I like him, for he is your friend—I think, a sincere one—and any one who is your friend, I cannot help liking.

"Oh! how I want to see you, if it was only for one hour, or even half that time. For one moment with you, I would be grateful to heaven. Concealment is vain—I will not suppress my feelings. I saw and loved you; but never intended you should know it. I do not ask for love in return, although nothing in the world would make me so happy. I know not where to stop. Is it impossible for me to see you? All, I hear, are excluded from seeing you; yet some do gain admittance. At least, you may write to me. For a single line, I would be grateful. Oh! could I see you again in freedom, I would not only be willing to be imprisoned, but to give up all I have and love on earth, to suffer every thing in the power of man to inflict; or to *die*. But alas! I cannot set you free. Ever Yours,

MIRANDA."

There! Such a letter as that might well repay one for a month's incarceration. It breathes Miranda's soul, a soul full of energy, yet so alive to every impulse of generous and tender feeling, that he must have a heart of ice, who could be unaffected by such disinterested—such *womanly* devotion. My passions, however ardent, are subdued, and can never hurry me faster than reason wills, yet reason tells me I should be grateful to Miranda, and love her, as well as so general and so platonic a lover can. And of this I must assure her in my letter—

TO MIRANDA.

Monday, June 24.

"My Dear Miranda:—As a ray of light, to the solitary and benighted wanderer, in desert wilds; as dainty viands, to the famished wretch; as a supporting plank tossed on the waves, within the reach of the shipwrecked and half drowned mariner, came your letter to my cell, where now I sit, from morn till eve, in solitude, and silence; or amid sounds, to which silence is a sweet relief.

"I read, and re-read it; and every time I perused it, I admired her, more and more, whose ingenuous spirit made her tear away the shackles of custom, which were never intended for noble natures, and from the fullness of her generous heart, pour out impassioned eloquence, and womanly love, and all the most devoted friendship could inspire. I am as proud as I am grateful. *One* does not forget me—one noble heart knows and loves me. But, I pray you, be not on my account unhappy. Never for me let pearly tears bedew the eyes of beauty. Far from being wretched or experiencing the horrors your active fancy has created, I live in a fairy world of romance, and revel in the pleasures of imagination. For once in my life, the present is almost a blank, and I live in the past and the future—the past, crowded with wild and beautiful incident—the future, brightened with glowing hopes of "fame, fortune, and happiness." Summon to your aid, then, all your philosophy, nor let the thoughts of this paltry imprisonment deprive you of one enjoyment within your reach. Oh! I would have you ever happy—you, and every bright being who has scattered flowers in my path of destiny, and helped to form the romance of my existence. Fate parts us now. We sit not beside each other; my arm cannot clasp your graceful form; our lips meet not in ambrosial kisses. Yet fancy me on a journey or absent in some distant city, but imagine me as happy as I can be, away from those I love, and fondly thinking of my return to their embraces.

" 'Tis not even so bad as that—for am I not here? do I not write to you? shall I not see you? and do you not know me well enough to be assured that no stretch of tyranny can overturn the equanimity of my temper, and that nothing *can* deprive me of my own internal power of enjoyment? Then grieve no more— and for your kind letter, and your generous feelings, may heaven bless you."

TUESDAY, JUNE 25, 1839.

A most beautiful morning. The sweet, balmy air came in through the grates of my prison, the bright sun shone on the lovely earth, and I heard the dear little birds singing gaily in the boughs of the trees. Pretty soon, my door was darkened by a female form, and a pair of sparkling eyes were looking at me, between the iron bars, and a kind and gentle voice, full of music, said—"Good morning, friend Nichols; come, get up; I am coming to see you pretty soon. The jailer says I may; and you may go up stairs"—and she vanished. Well now, what can have softened the jailer's heart? for yesterday, and day before, he would not allow her to come near my cell. Bright eyes? or bright gold? or a little of both? They are each powerful softners, but, combined, what can resist them? I never knew any thing that would.

Whatever may be the cause, he is uncommonly good to-day. My cell has scarcely been fastened, and I have had a number of visitors. There was Mr. W. with his big heart and whiskers, one of the few men here, whose souls are perceptible—men who do not cringe to vice seated on a money bag—who say with Pope,

"One, one man only, breeds my just offence;
Whose crimes gave wealth, and wealth gave impudence."

All but that first line, for it is not *"one man only"* here.

And a sweet lady has sent me some cake and some beautiful flowers. It is very kind of her. I so love flowers; and these have made me poetical—that is, rhythmical—and here is the consequence:

TO HER WHO SENT ME FLOWERS.

 Heaven bless thee, lady fair,—
  Thy kindness soothes the fleeting hours
   Of each departing day;
  And sweeter than the fragrant flowers,
   In all their colors gay,
  Sent by thy kindly care,
Is the fond thought, that such a heart as thine,
Feels sorrow for another's woes, and sympathy for mine.

 How welcome in this gloom,—
  Where nought falls on the listner's ear,.
   But clank of restless chains;
  Where all around me, palid fear
   And desperation reigns—
  The flowers' rich perfume!
But oh! fair lady, dearer far to me,
Is the blest thought, that still I live, fresh in thy memory.

My door was locked, and when my brunette came to see me, she stood on one side of the door and I on the other. Interesting position! One eye looked through one square space, and the other had to make use of the next one to it. Lord! how comical. I got up quite close to the grate—a curious magnetism got both our noses to playing checkers, and finally drew our four lips into one space, and —— it was but an experiment. I doubted if it were practicable. A true philosopher never loses an opportunity of ascertaining any new phenomenon. "Isn't it too bad?" said she. "Hem! not bad at all," I replied; but I dont know whether she meant it was too bad for her pouting lips to meet mine at all, or only because they could not do it more conveniently; so the experiment is not yet satisfactory, in all its details, but as far as it went, may be considered as one of the most interesting, in the whole range of philosophical investigation.

After dinner, a delicious dinner too, thanks to Mrs. C., I turned over a large bundle of exchange papers. Such a mass of trash. There were but three or four readable things in the lot. I cannot see the fun of publishing a paper, which it is a bore to read. The only news is that Mackenzie has been sentenced to eighteen months imprisonment in the Rochester jail. This is hard on Mackenzie, who is really less to blame for the Navy Island business, than fifty of the first men in Buffalo. He came here, and found the people all enthusiasm. They moved in the matter—he followed. They went and took possession of Navy Island, and he went after them. They had no business there; he had, for it was his country. But he is the victim. Mackenzie is brave, with an excess of both physical and moral courage, but rash, headstrong, opinionative, and imperative. He wants every thing his own way. Secretiveness and cautiousness cannot be among his phrenological developements. Combativeness, destructiveness, imperativeness, firmness and hopefulness are. I think I know Mackenzie well. At Toronto, he put himself at the head of a rabble of cowards, who at the first fire of the Loyalists, run as if the devil were after them. Mackenzie stood his ground, tried to rally them, begged, entreated, cursed, damned, and got into a terrible passion; but it was of no avail—they run, and he had to run too, to avoid being taken prisoner.

Some queer people call to see me. Strangers are admitted more freely than citizens, and none but those known to be my personal friends, or in my confidence, are rigidly excluded, or have not been to-day. My last caller was a real Job's comforter.

"Well, Nichols!" he said; "I tell you what it is, four months is a long while, I tell you. You are ruined now—you are totally used up. Why, Nichols, you are the best writer in this country. If you was out of jail, you might make ten thousand dollars! Now you will have to stay here. You will lose all your friends—they wont have nothing to say to you now—your paper will go down—you will lose all your subscribers. I am sorry for you!" And I burst into a long, loud, and very impolite fit of laughter. This is the first man who has said a doleful word, or done any thing but encourage me.

I am very industrious. Beside talking with those who are allowed to see me, reading, writing Journal; I yesterday copied eight long and beautiful letters, from one of my charming female correspondents, each a gem of a letter, and the whole series the most elegant that can be conceived. They extend through a space of several months, are anonymous, and to this day, I have only a surmise of who is the author.

One of my little girls has been scolding Sheriff Brown, for keeping me in jail; the dear one. I love little girls, and some large ones. How many persons I love! But then I love all that is lovely—all that is beautiful, all that is excellent. And in this naughty world there is a great deal to love. I love the glories of a summer morning, and the gorgeous splendor and beauty of our Buffalo sunsets. I love the sublime mountains, the beautiful valleys, the pleasant hills, the bright lakes and rivers of my native State. I love honesty, independence, and faith in man, and love, beauty and devotion in woman; and music, poetry, painting, sculpture, eloquence, and all the intellectual refinements and luxuries of life. Then I love a fine horse and a clever dog; also Champaigne and oysters; and steamboats I love hugely.

Gen. Scott is in town. Dr. Channing preached here last Sunday. George Combe is here, and Reverend Orville Dewey. They will not call to see me, and I cannot visit them. So much for being a prisoner.

Some of the ball and chain gang have been talking about literature, writing, arithmetic, etc. One indignant vagrant exclaimed, "Now I'd stop that; you had better take something warm and lay down!" That's what I call a good prescription.

The "Sun," edited by my friend the "Governor," still keeps up the excitement, condemns my persecutors and battles boldly for the right. "Governor" is the very imbodiment of honest independence. He fears no being, created or uncreated, bad or good; is an excellent printer, and an original, unshackled thinker. I like such men. You find one in every three thousand seven hundred and fifty six.

Monsieur Addrant, the little Magician, called to see me; and with him came a long-necked bottle, covered with lead foil, and looking wondrously like Champaigne wine. Monsieur knows something about magic. $ is the most powerful sign in the whole circle of the black art. It turns keys, opens doors, or knocks down stone walls. It confers respectability, and supplies the place of honor. It is the true object of our national worship; the sign of the divinity, in whose power none disbelieve; the foundation of a creed, whose faith is eminently practical, and which has fewer infidels than any other; and though this deity has an altar in every heart, it has its temples and its priesthood. The high priest of the orthodox sect has been Nick Biddle. Tom Benton is the leader of a new sect, or an old one revived, which is making great headway. One of its miracles is to make gold and silver swim up the Mississippi.

In Jail, June 26.

The sun is shining, warm and lovely. I see the reflection on yonder walls. I see the green grass growing up to meet it, glowing with life. The single branch of foliage in my sight is gently shaking in the morning breeze. Flowers are throwing their delicious perfume round the prisoner's cell. Thanks— a thousand thanks—to her whose goodness sent them.

I have been one week in prison. Fifteen weeks remain. If all pass as rapidly as the last, the time will not seem very long. But if the threats I hear, are put in execution—if I am deprived of every means of employment—if I am condemned, not only to imprisonment, but to idleness, the time may hang heavy on my hands. They cannot deprive me of my memory and thought; and these, in solitude and darkness, with chains on every limb, would make me happy—happier far than my persecutors, on their luxurious couches.

Change places with them? Not I, indeed—so shield me, Heaven. If there be another world, and future retribution, and I stood upon the gallows, with the rope about my neck, and just one moment of time allowed me before the drop fell, *then* I would not change places with any perjured, black-hearted, hypocritical scoundrel in existence! And if there be no hereafter, as I sometimes almost fear, even one hour of existence, with the proud consciousness of integrity, were better far than years of meanness, fraud, and crime. Talk not of changing places with such creatures as these.

The Sheriff has been here, and given orders more severe than ever. No one must see me, unless upon the most express and urgent business, which must be done in the presence of the jailer! I may have my food brought in, but it must be of the most plain and simple description. No luxuries—no nic-nacs, are to be allowed me. As if it made any difference what I eat!—as if the loss of freedom for one third of a year; the company of vagrants and felons; a miserable, filthy jail; a narrow, dark cell, close, hot, and swarming with vermin; and deprivation of society, the visits of friends, and all the ordinary comforts of life, were not enough!

Yet all this gratuitous severity and espionage, I laugh at. What does it avail? Do I write the less, or more mildly? Does it turn public sympathy from me? Will harsh and inhuman treatment deprive me of my friends? Will they make me a felon by treating me as one? Do they even succeed in giving me one hour's unhappiness? They are a little mistaken in the person they have to deal with. I have not only the spirit to bear my fate, and the worst of it, as becomes a man and a philosopher; but an ever-flowing fountain of joyous feeling, deep in my inmost soul, which no external circumstances can repress. I do not even know what it is to have what my fellow prisoners so often complain of, the 'horrors'; nor have I any definite notion of the meaning of the word. The President of a certain Bank has suffered more agony in one hour, from the exposure of his guilt and hypocrisy, than I should suffer, were every month of my imprisonment a year.

That coward creature knows what it is to suffer. I never saw or heard of a more truly contemptible person. Who does not remember, when, a few years ago, his conduct was exposed and censured at a public meeting, how the poor craven whined, and begged, and deprecated, and then fairly blubbered like a big, unwhipped baby, while crocodile tears ran down his sallow cheeks? Who has not seen him, time after time, in an agony of terror, when threatened with the consequences of his crimes? And even in reference to the endictments against me, and the possibility of his villanies coming to light, the poor creature has wept, and bitterly lamented that he suffered such men as P—— and C——, to urge him on. Who has not heard, how, when he was threatened with personal vengeance for some act of fraud, and thought the injured man was coming to his house, he begged his friends to protect him, and running up stairs, threw himself on his knees, and began to pray lustily to Heaven to save him—and all this time, it was a false alarm? And after he had, by his base treachery and corruption, secured his present office, how his guilty, wretched soul must have trembled, when, night after night, he surrounded his house with his minions, to guard him from expected vengeance! This *creature*, for I will not call him man—citizens of Buffalo, is YOUR MAYOR. Are you not *proud* of him? Do you not feel *honored* by being *bought* by him? The devil never flies over Buffalo in a thunder-gust, but he laughs so as to shake the steeples; and the bright angels, when they repose upon the edges of the glorious sunset clouds that are piled up by God's own hand in the western sky, and look down upon our beautiful city, weep pearly drops of heavenly pity for our shame. Oh! I could bear years of worse imprisonment than this, to wipe out that disgrace from a city I have chosen as my home.

TO A CERTAIN PRESIDENT, OF A CERTAIN BANK.

Banker! for life's last dread *return* prepare!
For no *false entry* can avail thee there—
Uncurrent bills wont make the balance even,
Nor *perjuries* pass thy sinful soul to heaven!

Thursday, June 27, 1839.

How reading the Boston Bard, should make me feel poetical and epigrammatic, of a rainy morning, when the condensed vapor of the upper regions is coming down in torrents, as if the spirits of air had served upon it a writ of ejectment; and when I am obliged to light a candle to read or write; is not easily accounted for. I perused the book because desired to, and because the prose part is readable—and skipped the poetry, as people will mine, if I ever am the monomaniac to publish it.

THE PRESS.

> Tyrants well know, they never can suppress,
> And shackle Freedom, till they bind the press;
> Guard sacred then, if ye would still be free,
> This proud palladium of your liberty.

That is unquestionably a fine sentiment, and must pass, maugre the rhymes of the first couplet. Try again.

EPIGRAM ON AN EDITOR.

> Corruption looked around for some fit tool,
> Easily led, and yet not quite a fool;
> Nature had left much malice and some soot—
> The dark ingredients mixed, and formed a F—te.

Severe, but just; though not more so than this—

ON A JUDGE.

Justice has fled—with streaming eyes,
These words I heard her utter;
"I've seen my representative
Lie, dead drunk, in a gutter."

The only merit of that, is its truth. A man is in a beautiful situation to hold the scales of justice, who, for a considerable portion of the time, is not able to support his own equilibrium!

A prisoner has been reading from the Bible, aloud, with a running commentary. "I cannot dig, to beg I am ashamed." "Then he will have to steal, or be put on the ball and chain gang for a vagrant." The succeeding operation, of the unjust steward cheating his master, was universally admired; and when he got out of the scrape, and was commended for his cunning, there was a general and very decided expression of approbation.

A Journal is disconnected, of necessity. I write a paragraph now—an hour hence, another; and in that time how many thoughts may have passed through my mind, each one suggesting another, until the next time I open my book, I strike off, on a theme as different as darkness from light.

I stopped to read a letter from Miranda. She says my letter made her very happy. Well; one was never made happy at a less expense. I wish I could make every body happy with a dash of my pen—but I wrong the dear girl, whom, though I admire, and love as well as so general and so platonic a lover can, I cannot understand. I cannot sympathize with the feelings which make her "laugh and weep alternately," at the thought of seeing me, when she did not expect to. Woman, verily, is a mystery. Miranda writes eloquently, and I think sincerely.

"Oh! if you could but for one moment imagine how very unhappy I have been—how often, at the silent hour of midnight, when all has been hushed and still, I have sat at my window, and watched the soft blue sky, and the twinkling stars, and prayed, earnestly prayed, to Him who made us and them, for your liberation, you would rather pity than blame me." * * * * * "Do you think I could get weary of writing to you? I could write, talk, and think of you, for hours, days, weeks, and months; **and so** far from making me weary it would still be a pleasure." * * * *

"I would to God, I was, in myself, an army strong and powerful—the sun should not set again in the west, before you should be free. Oh! when I think of your being shut up in a prison, deprived of the fresh air of heaven, of the society of your friends, and Liberty, which is dearer than all, to a mind like yours I feel as if I had rather—much rather, die than live."

I cannot tell whether this gave me more pain or pleasure, for I read it with mingled emotions. While it gratified my adhesiveness and love of approbation, speaking in a fashion phrenologically pedantic, my organ of kindness was affected disagreeably,—and I wrote the following—

LINES TO MIRANDA.

Be happy—such a heart as thine,
    Should never beat to aught but pleasure;
Let it throb gaily now as mine,
    Which still keeps time to joyous measure.

Be happy—see, the clear bright sky
    And beauteous earth with joy are beaming;
Shall sorrow dim thy brighter eye,
    While round thee laughing sunlight's streaming?

Wilt thou be sad when all are gay,
    And smiles from Nature's face are glancing?
When all around thee, night and day,
    Spirits of bliss are ever dancing?

Be happy—I entreat, implore,
  Command; for love makes joy a duty!
And for my luckless fate no more
  May sorrow dim the eyes of beauty.

I should explain, that it had cleared off, previous to this; and the sunlight was coming down with such a joyous *slantindicularity*, and the rain drops were glittering so *diamonically*, as made me happy to look at.

A writer in the Republican, who has been dealing savagely with Pratt, in the course of his article calls me a *"boy editor."* I should like to know how old one must be, to be a man. These gray-beards think all are boys, who are under fifty. How old was Alexander, surnamed the Great, when, placing himself at the head of his father's veteran troops, he led them to the conquest of Persia, and commenced that brilliant career which made his name immortal? How old was Wm. Pitt, when he became Premier of England and covered his country with debt and glory? How old was Napoleon, when he took the command of the Army of Italy and commenced his bloody, victorious march to empire and endless renown? How old was Lafayette, when he embarked from the shores of France, to fight the battles of American freedom? *Boy Editor!*

I am "inexperienced," too. Since I was eleven years old, I have educated myself. For ten years I have mingled with the world, in town and country, and mixed with, and *studied* every class of society. For five years I have been connected with the press. Indeed, I can scarcely remember the time when I was not acting in some sort, in a public capacity. As a school-boy even, and the youngest of two hundred pupils, I was the champion of the school-boy's rights; and won the regard of my preceptor, by my bold defence of them, and opposition to his tyranny: for though a good, and a learned man, he was a tyrant. I admired his virtues, but ever detested that vice. And how I pitied the meanness of those, my seniors, who crouched and quailed before him, as I would before no created being—no! nor *any* being; for I was not made in the image of God, to cringe and quiver, like a mean and guilty wretch. Eternal ages of torture should not bring my soul to that.

Once, I took a powerful drug, and thought I woke in hell. It was many years ago; but I well remember how calmly I folded up my arms, and waited for the tortures to begin, and determined to bear them through eternity, so that the very devils would respect me. Do the idiots, who have thrust me into this cell, think they can make me succumb, or give up one particle of my independence? They are poor, pitiful, coward knaves; and judge me by themselves!

Mr. Sheriff Brown has called, and says the Secretary of State wishes for some information in regard to me; and propounding the following questions, received the following answers:

"What is your age?"

"Twenty-three."

"Your place of birth?"

"Orford, Grafton county, Newhampshire."

"Are both your parents living?"

"Yes."

"What are your domestic relations—married, or single?"

"Single."

"What has been your degree of mental cultivation?"

"Fair to middling, thank you."

"Your habits of life, in regard to temperance?"

"Temperate."

"Yes; I believe I can testify to that. Well, Mr. Nichols, I believe that is all. Good evening."

"Good evening, sir."

JAIL, JUNE 28, 1839.

The Buffalonian came this morning, full of errors; and some of the articles mangled horribly. How many curses have been heaped upon printers, by the irritable genus of scribblers! A compositor must spell, punctuate, and correct the grammatical construction of his author's sentences.

They tell of Rathbun coming home in July. How strange, if he should, and find me in his old cell! I should be glad to see him. There are few men of this age, whose fate and genius are so remarkable as those of Benjamin Rathbun. Allowing him to be a criminal; what were the motives which actuated him? So far as I can understand them, from a full and minute examination of all the evidence which has been made public, it was to save a brother and two nephews from disgrace, or the State Prison; to prevent the distress that must come upon thousands who looked to him for bread; to prevent all his stupendous schemes of improvement being crushed in the bud, and protect the interests of his creditors, and those of the city, of which he had been the architect; for Rathbun made all of Buffalo that is worth looking at. And all this he would have done, but for the treachery of the scoundrels, who fawned around him, and promised to support him through all, until they had his immense property in their power, and who then fell upon him, utterly helpless as he was, crushed him to the earth, took posession of his estate, used the very means his enterprise and genius had accumulated to send him to prison, or appropriated it, not to the payment of his creditors, but to their own agrandizement. The whole course of Rathbun shows him to have been the most honest man connected with the business. He literally fell among thieves.

The influence of this set of men upon Buffalo, has been demoralizing to the last degree. There is not a city in the union where the tone of moral sentiment is so low, or the laws of honor and the principles of justice so little regarded; and for the truth of this observation, I fearlessly appeal to all the honest portion of the community. Things which in any other place, that I was ever in, would produce the most intense excitement, here pass almost without notice and almost as a matter of course, and acts, for which a man, in Arkansas would be lynched by the populace, and perhaps hung up on the most convenient tree, are here the cause of a jest.

To counteract this influence, to awaken a higher

tone of moral feeling, to excite sentiments of honor, has been the object of my labors; and like all reformers, I am persecuted, and like many, imprisoned. It is not strange. I want no better evidence of the correctness of my conduct than the malignant hatred of the scoundrels who have been the cause of my incarceration!

A little army of boys and girls has assembled in the court house. How merrily rings their laughter! The lovely little girls, too, Heaven bless their bright eyes. I suppose they are Sunday scholars, preparing for their celebration of the Fourth of July. What a wild hurra was that! Do they look down here, I wonder, and think of me? I'll be sworn the little girls do—I am sure of it.

I ever loved little girls. Many years ago, when I was a schoolboy, of some twelve or fourteen summers, a lovely little angel was a playmate of mine for a day or two. She was a rare creature; beautiful as the light, and gentle as beautiful. I feel even now, the soft thrill of delight that went over me, when she took my hand, and in the spirit of guileless affection with which her little bosom was overflowing, pressed it to her rosebud lips. Heaven never smiled on a holier feeling, than that with which I folded the charming little fairy to my heart. Where is she now? I know not—I cannot even remember her name; but when I go to the world of bliss above, I shall look round among its blessed inhabitants, for that lovely little girl!

Since Mackenzie has got into Jail, and as I believe, so unjustly, I take quite an interest in his fate.

"A fellow feeling makes us wondrous kind!"

He feels irritated, and chafes like a caged tiger. I will send him this box of salve—it may soothe his irritation, though composed only of "simple cerate," with the addition, perhaps, of a few grains of "soft sawder."

TO WM. L. MACKENZIE, IN PRISON.

Bear patiently, Mackenzie! each reverse—
Think, better men have oft been treated worse;
Posterity will right thee yet, and long
Thy name shall live, in story and in song.

Thy dauntless courage, perseverance, zeal—
Thy deep devotion to thy country's weal—
These are the virtues shall inscribe thy name,
In living light, upon the scroll of Fame.

T. L. N.

Buffalo Jail, Convict's Cell, June 28.

SATURDAY JUNE, 29.

The glorious Fourth is fast approaching. Again, cannon will be fired, flags raised, orations pronounced, dinners eaten, and wine drunk, with patriotic toasts and music. So be it.

And at night, bonfires will illumine the steeples, rockets will rush toward heaven, fire balls will bound through the streets, fire wheels whiz, and serpents hiss. Let them.

It is a proud and glorious day, and ever may it be celebrated; but can our citizens forget, in the festivities of that day, that in this city, of all the rights for the support of which the Declaration of Independence was signed, and in defence of which our fathers fought and bled, we have scarcely one remaining? The elective franchise—the choice of our rulers, has been rendered a nullity, by an infamous *clique*. The freedom of the press has been assailed. The administration of the laws has been made a mockery of justice. Corruption reigns supreme over law—and tyrannic usurpation sets public opinion at defiance. So much for the day we celebrate.

I shall lose the pleasure of the excursion to Detroit, with the City Guards and Frank Johnson's "famed brass band." That is not all. I lose the splendid excursion to the upper lakes and *Sault St. Marie*, in the beautiful steamer Chesapeake, which I had promised myself, and her captain, in July. It is a magnificent excursion. There is nothing on the earth like the clear waters and wild scenery of the upper part of Lake Huron.

Mr. W. this morning brought me the Letters of Junius. I have read them through, more carefully than ever before, pencil in hand, and have copied some of the most striking passages. Whoever may have been the author, and I have taken no interest in the investigation, nor cared to know by what name men called him, he was deeply inbued with the spirit of liberty; and for that I honor him.

"Never," says he, "suffer an invasion of your political constitution, however minute the instance may appear, to pass by, without a determined, persevering resistance: one precedent creates another—they soon accumulate, and constitute law. '

Nor less truly does he remark, that "good men consult their piety as little as their judgment and experience, when they admit the great and essential advantages, accruing to society from the freedom of the press, yet indulge themselves in peevish or passionate exclamations against the abuses of it."

He would "promote and encourage a constant examination into the conduct of public officers and magistrates." And with what force does the sentiment that "he, who by secret corruption, invades the freedom of elections, and the ruffian, who by open violence destroys that freedom, are embarked in the same bottom," come home to us! Nor less the following:

"We have seen the laws, sometimes scandalously relaxed; sometimes violently stretched beyond their tone;" and—

"Have not the first rights of the people, and the first principles of the constitution been openly invaded, and the very name of an election made ridiculous?"

How many men are there among us, "who, affecting a character of moderation, in reality consult nothing but their own immediate ease; who are weak enough to acquiesce, under a flagrant violation of the laws, when it does not directly touch themselves, and care not what injustice is practised upon a man, whose moral character they piously think themselves obliged to condemn!"

And I would have our Judges remember, what the infamous Stryker forgot, or did not regard, that "when they invade the province of the Jury in matter of libel, they in effect, attack the liberty of the press." Nor is it less true, that "Jurymen are too often ignorant of their own rights, and too apt to be awed by the authority of a Judge."

Some men in this community shall be fully convinced, that "Deliberate treachery entails punishment upon the traitor. There is no possibility of escaping it, even in the highest rank to which the consent of society can exalt the meanest and worst of men!"

Junius does not think well of lawyers. He says "the indiscriminate defence of right and wrong, contracts the understanding, while it corrupts the heart." Yet our halls of legislation are filled with lawyers. While an honest lawyer—I mean a lawyer who is an *honest man*—is a *rara avis*, at the same time no one deserves more of society. The strength of principle, necessary for such a character; the union of firmness and conscientiousness in such powerful developement, as Professor Grimes would say, is as rare as it is excellent; but it is doubtless generally true of the profession, that "subtlety is mistaken for wisdom, and impunity for virtue"; and with the mass of mankind, it is not, I fear, very different.

There! Junius is pretty well picked over.

7 *

Sunday, in Jail.

The Holy Sabbath has come again; my second in prison. Once, I hear, they used to have service; some Minister of Christ, or pious lay brother, used to come and talk with the prisoners and make a prayer. It was but an awkward business, and they have given it up. All the prisoners were locked in their cells, and the preacher or exhorter was obliged to stand in some corner, where he could see nobody, and raise his voice, so as to penetrate forty iron-doored cages. There was no fun in this. How could he tell what effect he was producing upon his auditors? It was like a blindfolded blacksmith, hammering away to no purpose; so now, the only difference, between Sunday and other days, is that we are more closely confined to our cells.

A friend writes me, from the world of sunlight and freedom, that "The best feeling prevails, both in regard to you, and the paper. The matter is ripe in the country. All the people are your friends. Stryker is forever down, and there is talk of tarring and feathering the District Attorney. From what I can hear, there is but one state of feeling, pervading all this section of country—that is sympathy, admiration and friendship for you; and hatred of your persecutors—of Hiram and his whole gang, down to the loafers in his employ. Every body says you are in a fair way to be the greatest man in all this Western country; and I incline to believe them."

And so, perhaps, I am, in my own opinion; but not exactly in the way they wish to have me. They talk of my going to Congress, running for Assembly; and swear I shall be Mayor of Buffalo next spring. Fudge! I shall run for neither office. I want neither. By Heaven! I would not put myself on a level with the rascally politicians, by running against them. I might be prevailed upon to run against Hiram Pratt, were there no one else, but scarcely otherwise. I don't want office. No man ever had less ambition of that sort. When a public servant faithfully performs his duties, and displays honesty and ability, I esteem him; but I have no desire to let myself out, either to make laws or execute them. Some men's itch for office is, to me, unaccountable.

My cell has no Bible, and mine did not come with my other books. I feel as if one of Solomon's Songs, or a chapter in Revelations would be refreshing. It is wonderful to me, why we have no metrical version of these most beautiful Songs of the wisest of monarchs, and most splendid and glorious. I cannot help admiring a man who had three hundred wives and seven hundred concubines. There is a sort of sublimity in such a man's domestic fireside. All wise men love pretty women; but none have come up to the inspired monarch of Israel. When he spake of the vanity of worldly grandeur, it must have been in his hours of quiet enjoyment, when he had laid aside the cares of state, and, in the bosom of his family, was enjoying the sweets of domestic felicity.

JULY 1, 1839.

JAMES GORDON BENNETT, ever fearless and independent, has come out upon the subject of my conviction. So, to be sure, have most of the Eastern and Southern and Western papers. Here is the article from the Herald.

LIBERTY OF THE PRESS IN BUFFALO.—Nichols, the editor of the "Buffalonian," has been found guilty of a libel, in publishing that some person was the tool of another. The libel, as it is called, was published during Nichols' absence from Buffalo, when he had no personal control over his paper. On this libel he has been tried, found guilty, imprisoned four months, and fined $150. He is now in jail, and his jailer is authorized by the authorities of Buffalo, to prevent him from writing for his paper.

This case of Nichols' presents a most curious affair—perfectly *unique* in the history of the press in this country. We do not know that any despotic government in Europe, ever showed such tact, unscrupulousness, and audacity, in shackling the press, as the legal authorities of Buffalo have exhibited. With juries, judges, and public officers, under the influence of a *clique* of persecutors, the liberty of the press can be as effectually destroyed in Buffalo as in Petersburg or Pottsdam. Not long ago a pair of Swiss minstrels were imprisoned in Buffalo for singing some of their mountain airs, and we should not be surprised to hear of some man clapt into jail for the cut of his coat, or size of his hat.

On the subject of Nichols' fine, we have only a word to say. Let us here understand the real character of this transaction, and if, as we are disposed to think he has been persecuted by a *clique* of bad men, whose deeds would not bear the light, we will open a subscription, and raise the money to pay his fine, and shall put down our own name, at the head of the list for $20 to begin with.

That is characteristic. The world does not know Bennett. I know, and appreciate him. For some four months, I was with him several hours, every day. He is an extraordinary man, in every respect. Few men in this country, have acquired such a fund of information. He talks, when he does talk, which is seldom, even better than he writes, and every body knows that he writes as few others can. What a strange blunder those made, who used to say, as a left handed compliment, that I wrote like Bennett. Nor was it true, in fact. I can write like him, the same as I can imitate any writer—Irving, Willis, Neal; Bulwer, D'Israelli, Dickens, &c. &c. The faculty of imitation applies as well to writing, as to any thing else. Any one who has it, if, after choosing his subject, he will read a few pages of the author he wishes his style to resemble, can imitate it without difficulty. I will engage to write successful imitations of any twenty that can be selected in half a day. I have written a sketch in imitation of H. H. Welde, to which his name was affixed, without scruple, by the papers in which it was copied. My paragraphs *a la Bennett* have been copied with his, as specimens of his style, and so on.

Mackenzie don't like being in jail. Speaking of the Jail at Rochester, said to be far superior to this, he says—

"The jail at Toronto is a palace, compared to this! When Francis Collins was sent a year to it for libel on the Government, he got two of the best rooms in the prison, handy to the outer door, his types and cases were brought into the prison, and his wife lived there with him. Humanity there allowed to all a spacious yard for health!

"Dodge and Theller had daily exercise for hours, on the ramparts of Quebec, though the latter had been condemned for High Treason.

"The Prescott prisoners after sentence of death had been passed upon them, had the use of nearly five acres of parade ground—and even Lafayette, in his dungeon of Olmutz, took an occasional ride over the prison grounds."

These examples are in pleasant contrast with my treatment here, yet worse is threatened. The scoundrels want me to get down on my knees to them. If I dont have them *vice versa* before a year is well over, it will not be because I make no effort.

Tuesday, July 2, 1839.

Two weeks in jail! With what a zest shall I enjoy freedom, when once more at liberty; and yet, I like it well enough here. I read, and write. I get letters and answer them. Miranda writes me beautiful and eloquent ones. Those of Julia are as much so, but not so passionate; at least there is not such an abandonment of feeling. She is subdued, calm, lady like and philosophical. Yet it is strange how similar emotions produce similar expressions. She writes—

"My Dearest N:—We are not allowed to visit you, and I have therefore invented this plan of sending you a note. I know not that you will get it, but I can but make the attempt.

"When I first heard of your close confinement, and that you were not even allowed to see a friend, I uttered an exclamation of surprise, while tears filled my eyes, that compelled me to withdraw, for fear of observation. I cannot, indeed, hear your name mentioned without feeling agitated. Oh! you little know how unhappy I am at this moment. I am scarcely able to conceal the anguish of my soul. Only think! four long months immured in solitude! I cannot, indeed, become reconciled to it.

"We often made your going to jail a theme of conversation; but I could never bring it to my mind that it was possible for those tyrants to send you there; but so it is, and they think they can do what they please, and set public opinion at defiance; but there must come a day of retribution. The citizens of Buffalo will not tolerate such proceedings. Be patient, and all will soon be right.

"How lonely I am. Here I sit, waiting, and looking; for what I know not. You are confined and cannot come to see me, yet I am every moment expecting to see you, coming to pass an hour with me. When am I to see you again? Weeks will appear months, and months years, until I do." * * *

I know not what magic there may be, which makes

me friends among the gentle and lovely sex. I am very far from being a "lady's man,"—I am not a coxcomb—I never think of dress—and I am the soul of candor. I never flatter, I never went "a courting" in my life, and am much too indolent, or indifferent to make love to any one. I despise a male coquette; but rather like a female one; and do not think a man, whose heart one could injure, deserving of pity. I am no gallant—never dance, never ride with ladies, attend no parties, make no gossiping calls, and am very badly qualified for a *cavalier servante*. Beside all this, I am but tolerably good looking.

Yet for all that, I have acquired the reputation, the Lord knows how, for no one was ever more innocent of it, of using every art of seductive flattery, and of being something very near an accomplished rake: when every one, who is acquainted with me, knows that I am the plainest hearted mortal living, and little less than a palpable personification of the great principle of McDowalism and moral reform. I hope this may never fall into the hands of any of my readers of the Buffalonian, who "like it, all but its egotism." Good Heavens! if that were taken away, I wonder what there would be left! The advertisements?

I have more friends among the married ladies than the single, and that's queer, too. They are not those who have marriageable daughters, for I am not of the marrying sort, nor a desirable match. Any blockhead, or even a blackguard with a few thousands in possession or expectation, would be a better one; but I never would, and never will, allow a married lady to write me confidential letters—for if I have a horror of any thing, it is the least ground for suspicion of crim. con. And if I were to give my most serious and important advice to all the married ladies in christendom—women are not taught to write any where else—in just two words, they would be, "never write." Letters will miscarry. They will get intercepted. Lovers will be careless, husbands will be jealous, and then there is the devil to pay. I never received a letter from a married woman, that could by any means be construed into a *billet doux*, without a perilous trepidation; and immediately that the organs near it had received the benefit of its contents, destructiveness was aroused, and the scented, gilt edged, little innocent looking missive was consigned to the flames. Truly wrote some sensible sinner—"When the devil wishes to ruin a woman, he puts a pen in her fingers." All this applies not to misses, nor widows, to Julia nor Miranda, to Constanza nor Rosalie.

Wednesday, July 3, 1839.

MALEDICTIONS.

Loud the shout of triumph rose,
    When the cause of Freedom fell,
And, where fire infernal glows,
    Demons echoed it in hell!
Hypocrites were broadly grinning,
    Underneath their solemn masks;
They, whom fear had kept from sinning,
    Now resumed their guilty tasks;
Corruption reigned; by cursed gold
Justice was bribed, and Freedom sold.

O liberty! thou sacred name,
    What sacrilege to call thee ours,
When all the rights that freemen claim
    Are in the dust, and o'er them towers
Usurping tyranny and wrong,
Outrage, fraud and crime, that long,
With strange impunity, has trod,
Like thieves of old, the courts of God!
Oh! grossest crimes are sheltered there
By solemn look and mocking prayer!

> Where are thy red lightnings, Heaven?
> Where the thunders of thy wrath,
> When thy chariot wheels are driven
> O'er the clouds' majestic path?
> Shall the guilty triumph ever?
> Can the God of Justice still
> Bear with them, and will they never,
> Their deep cup of vengeance fill?
> God of vengeance! let them perish
> By the vipers they have nursed!
> By the demons that they cherished,
> Let their guilty souls be cursed!

And tomorrow is the Fourth of July. How different from the celebration a year ago, when I was enjoying every scene of festivity and revelry. Tomorrow I shall celebrate by myself in a convict's cell; still am I happy.

The cells were washed out this morning, and I paid a visit to the debtors' apartments, in the upper story of the jail. Here are plenty of rooms, comparatively comfortable. We played a game of whist. Poor fellows—for the crime of being in debt and unable to pay, and not being citizens of the Empire State, they are no sooner caught within its boundaries, than they are thrust into prison. A most inhospitable statute, and a bad way of taking in strangers. In the mean time, their business may be deranged, their families may suffer. Their creditors are relentless—the county is obliged to board them; and after lying in jail for months, half fed, and miserably provided for, they take advantage of the act, and are released. The creditor has gratified his devilish malice, and all the rest are sufferers. And yet this man goes to church every Sunday, sits at the communion table, and prays, "Forgive us our debts as we forgive our debtors!"

Bill Smith is a cool one. Though but a mere boy, of seventeen or thereabout, he is a hard covie. Barton sent him four months on the ball and chain gang, for gambling! He got out four days ago, and to-day was sent back again for another month. Never did mortal take a matter more coolly. He sat down and had an eighteen pound shot with a chain some two feet long, riveted to his ankle, took possession of his old quarters, and eat his dish of mush and molasses for supper.

"How came you to get caught again so soon?" said I.

"Why I was d——d careless;" he replied. "I went into the back room of a grocery to play a game of 'seven up' with a fellow, for half a dollar, and I was just cursed fool enough to let the half dollar lay on the table, when the constable came in and caught us at it.

You see, if the money hadn't been there, he wouldn't have known but we were playing for fun."

Bill is a victim of circumstances. Were he capable of going into Wall street, and gambling in stocks—or speculating in fancy lots; if he could get up a red-back bank, or under the cover of respectability, bet on elections or fast trotting horses; in short, could he contrive to swindle fashionably and on a large scale, he would be in no danger of the ball and chain gang, and of being driven out upon the high ways, thus manacled, to labor.

And with what propriety, I should like to know, can James L. Barton sentence a boy to an ignominious punishment, for such a crime?

Holland started for Auburn, to-day; poor fellow! He does not look like a villain. I did not think they would convict him; but it is impossible to form any opinion of the verdict of a jury. The weather is easier to prognosticate. One of the jury that found me guilty came in to see me yesterday. He said the charge of the Judge was all that made them convict me. The last man they brought over, was an old Dutchman. He held out manfully, until he got very sleepy. "Py cot," he said; "these fellows got that man ash did sho much for Puffalo, and shent him to states prishon; and now, if dis leetle poy can do any goot mit his leetle paper, he shall do it py cot!" But it was very late, and he got very sleepy. The eleven got round him, and made him believe Stryker's charge was law. He wanted to go home to his farm and vrow, gave up the contest—and I am in jail. So much for a jury.

My spirits, always overflowing in a tide of happiness, burst the narrow bounds that would now confine them. I walk in the jail yard, when allowed to. To-day I took a long march—thirty feet, and "right about face"—then I lay down upon the grass, and looked up to the sky; for on every side the high stone walls prevent any prospect of sublunary scenes, and sung. It was no doleful ditty, nor song of captive knight, but all the merry lays I could think of; such as

"Am not I, am not I, say, a merry Swiss boy?"

And then I sung,

"Oh! delightful hour,
I'm in pleasure's bower,
Every where a flower,
　Springs up in my way."

Or—

"Happy am I, from care I'm free;
Why are not all contented like me?"

And then I sung,

"I'd be a butterfly , born in a bower."

But by this time, down came all the robbers, thieves, counterfeiters and vagrants; a motley crew; some ragged and filthy to the last degree, some with the appearance and bearing of gentlemen—some doubtless guilty, others beyond question innocent of crime; each with his brown earthen pitcher in his hand, which he fills from a shallow well, furnished with a chain and bucket, the water of which would be good, were it clean, and did not the idea of the horrid creatures that draw from it disgust one. I can almost see the vermin with which they are covered, drop into the water as they bend over it. I never thought to be a companion of human beings, to whom I have to give a wide berth when they pass me, and avoid getting to the leeward of them. One of them took off his jacket, one day, and threw it on the grass. I took my eyeglass, and a long stick, to examine it. I turned it over, and for the first time in my life, saw the reptiles. They were as large as kernels of wheat, and the old jacket was completely covered! Many of the cells, and even the upper rooms and bedding, swarm with them. Bugs infest the whole building, in innumerable armies. Blood-thirsty and ferocious, they crawl upon you by hundreds; they ascend the wall, and drop down upon you from the ceiling. Clean linen, perfumes and poisons mitigate the evil; but these are but a partial remedy. Rats and mice swarm around me in countless numbers. They eat my bread and cake, and get drowned in my water jug. Such is the jail of Erie county—such are some of the pleasures of an imprisonment.

> Fly along, ye wheels of time!
>   Ye never can revolve too fast;
> Why should I waste here youth's bright prime,
>   Wishing each lagging hour the last?
>
> Let me sigh for stores of wealth,
>   Wish vainly other lands to see;
> In sickness let me long for health;
>   But never languish to be free!

IN PRISON, FOURTH OF JULY, 1839.

Independence in prison! The fourth of July in a County Jail! Not one moment out, and for the most of the day shut up in my cell. I *cell*-ebrated as Benton kicked the ball, "solitary *and* alone."

Early on Wednesday evening, I began to hear an occasional note of preparation,—the whiz of the rocket—the sharp crack of the pistol, and multitudinous fire crackers, with the ringing shouts of merry, independent boys. As the shades of night thickened around me, so did these joyous precursors of our Nation's Festival, until towards midnight, matters had reached a high pitch of patriotic enthusiasm.

I tried to sleep. It was a cloudy night and a close air. Sleep was insensibly creeping over me—but that was not all. Too sensibly I felt that others had claims upon me, or would have in a short time, for they seemed determined to make a settlement.

The spirit of seventy-six was roused within me. I made horrid havoc, and killed enough to gain two or three national victories. I am not, naturally, of a bloody disposition, but I felt wronged. There was nothing of the kind in my sentence. The lately pure linen was re-smoothed, re-sprinkled with cologne, and I lay down to sleep—"perchance," etc.

Again I was attacked, again repulsed the foe; regiment after regiment lay routed, and "the cry was still they come!"

>"Still so gently o'er me stealing,
>Memory will bring the feeling,"
>After all that I've been killing,
>   That they bite me—bite me still!

Hark! Again, and again that wild hurra! Now it comes nearer—it is—"Hurra for Nichols—bang!" Here's glory! The hurra—bang! was the last sound that I heard. Sleep closed my eyelids. I dreamed.

I stood upon the field of battle, and my sword, drenched in blood, stuck to my hand; the stripes and stars were floating above me; the dead and dying were around. The foe were flying, and in my ear rang the peal of cannon and cheers of victory. I awoke with the sound of many voices around me. There was no mistake about the cannon, nor the shouts. They rose again. "Three cheers for Thomas L. Nichols! Hurra! Hurra! Hurra!" For them I am obliged to my patriotic fellow citizens, the "peep of day boys"—for Aurora was just showing the tip of her nose in the East. The bells rung out their merry peals at sunrise, and the deep-mouthed cannon carried the exulting notes of freedom far into the dominions of her Majesty, Victoria. The uproar increased. Stirring strains of martial music vibrated the air of my prison. I saw the gleaming files of glittering bayonets, the polished cannon, the waving plumes, and the proud banners fluttering in the morning breeze. The procession moved on. In fancy, I saw it enter the Temple of Jehovah.

I saw too—in the green groves—beneath the shady trees—manly pride and woman's glorious beauty. There were

> "Glancing eyes—like sudden gleams,
> That glow through autumn clouds."

And wandering in those lonely shades, whose boughs were—

> "Bending beneath the invisible west wind's sighs,"

were seen, here and there,

> "Creatures so bright that the same lips and eyes
> They wear on earth, will serve for Paradise."

And they listened with rapture to those

> "Words of sunshine—'*Freedom to the world!*'"

Light, loveliness, and Liberty. were all about them. They were in Freedom's Sanctuary, and all felt

> "Those god-like breathings in the air
> "Which mutely told her spirit had been there."

And then the evening's scene of splendor and beauty.

We saw it not with our bodily eye—but it is glittering, in gorgeous loveliness, on fancy's canvass—nor so cold and stiff as that. What we imagine, is more real than a picture. It is the glowing creation of the Ideal.

Thus has passed the Glorious Fourth. And it is a glorious day. The signing of the Declaration of Independence was sublime. Sublime are the principles of human rights it contains; but how are they regarded!

IN JAIL, JULY 5.

The novelty of the thing has worn away—I have settled down to the sameness of an every day life in prison. I see every day the same four walls of one little "cubby hole" of a cell—the same checkered iron door—the same little patch of green grass, and the four inches square of blue sky. Life passes with the same unvarying round, and yet, singular as it may appear, the first day seemed like this, and this seems in every thing like the first; and, stranger, still I like it, even better than I expected.

I never was happier. I never was busier. I scarcely allow myself time for exercise and rest. I read and write, from morning till night; and when for a few moments I walk in the yard, I return impatient to my task, which task is a pleasure, the richest, and but one, the dearest. They wished to take away my books and paper. Let them. I should be happy still. I defy human ingenuity to prevent my being so. I fear not—I never despair—I never regret. Sympathy and pity, for me, are as good as thrown away. There are thousands out of prison who need it far more than I. There *are* objects of pity. The man who walks about the streets, with a face pallid from the agonies of fear and remorse, and the ever-biding consciousness that he is *detested*, is to be pitied more than I. The man who by a paltry bribe was induced to outrage the laws he was sworn to administer and support—the perjured minister of holy justice, who has made her sacred name a mockery, and himself a miserable minion of corruption, is a pitiable object. Far more are those unfortunate beings, who are bound to them by ties, the tenderest and dearest, who, innocent themselves, yet suffer all the shame of guilt. Pity them. I need no pity. I'll have none. Pity me? Why, there are not ten persons in this city with whom I would change places. I doubt, indeed, if there be one. So, enough of pity.

It is a question I often ask myself—Am I deceived in respect to the people of this city? I am not convinced of it yet. I have given them credit for being liberal, generous, noble-minded, patriotic, persevering; in short, for being all that the citizens of one of the finest and most prosperous young cities of this nation, should be. I should be sorry to be mistaken. I'll not believe it possible—and yet, there are some very strange things.

In no other city but Buffalo, could Hiram Pratt be Mayor. In no other city could I be imprisoned under the same circumstances. In no city is corruption and crime in high places, so reckless and so triumphant. These are all bad pictures, but I look every day for the commencement of revolution and reform. I wait to have the people of this city act like themselves, and show to the world that I have not mistaken them, nor thought and spoken of them better than they merit.

In this hope I shall persevere, as I have begun, battling with villany and corruption, until silenced by force. In this cause I am proud to suffer. There is no selfishness in the case. Had I consulted pecuniary interests and personal popularity, I should have made friends with these rogues long since. Nor have I been controlled, nor in any manner influenced, by others. What I have done, I wish to have all the credit of, and all the blame. The credit, I mean, for disposition; for, in ability, I have received important assistance. What I wish to disavow is, being the instrument or the dupe of any man. Let the course I have taken, and its final results, be witnesses.

A party of visiters has been looking at me through my door. There were citizens and country cousins. All were curious to see how I looked, and to know how I felt. It was too dark for the former, and I am cheerful always. They pitied, condoled, and departed. I made a pitcher of iced lemonade, which I am sipping from my silver goblet; for I drink from plate, and I read Bulwer's Asmodeus.

I am conscious that I write badly. How can I avoid it. There is a perfect row—a noisy row, all the time—a most blackguardly, ferocious row. If "evil communications corrupt good manners," I shall be exceedingly corrupt, and most unmannerly. No lady has come to see me for two days,—none that I know and love. I have had no letters. It is an awful thing to shut up a set of men together, with no women. What a set of cut-throats the human race would be without them. I never believed in separating the sexes. Separate schools for boys and girls I detest. They ought to grow up and be educated together. Separation is bad for both. It is wrong and unnatural. A school should be like a family. Boys and girls should love one another like brothers and sisters. They should study, work, and play together. They assist and check each other. A boy must be very wicked, and very hardened, to use unseemly language in the presence of a beautiful girl. He never will, unless he has been brutalized by being herded with those of his own sex.

A Dutch boy has been committed for stabbing another. Both were in love with the same girl, and in a fit of jealousy Michael stabbed his rival, but did not wound him dangerously; and now he walks the yard for hours. He looks dejected. It is a bad business, and may send him to State Prison. He gets much sympathy, especially from the Dutch girls.

SATURDAY, JULY 6, 1839.

LETTER TO ROSALIE.

"MY DEAR ROSALIE:—I don't know as you will feel yourself particularly honored by having a letter written to you from a prisoner's cell; nor very much flattered with the *commencement* of what I am, with permission of the jailer, about to inflict upon you. I wrote it before I thought—that is, before I took my "sober second thought;" and I am, very much in the habit of beginning letters with 'my dear,' which in some cases means no more—but I see I am getting myself deeper at every flounder; so, my dear, you must let it go 'my dear,' without further apology; and if you *are* offended, it will be a sensation; and that, in this world of sameness and *ennui,* is *something:* so, whether it please or displease you, you will be the gainer; and if, as I soberly suppose—for I keep very sober now, from necessity—it be a matter of indifference, nothing is lost, but the time you spend in reading it.

"Do you perceive what I am at? I write to pass time, to fancy I am not alone, to imagine I am looking into your eyes, and talking to you. I write because I would write to some one, and that some one should be a lady; and you, for the moment—not very gallant, but I can't help it—*happened* to be uppermost in my mind; and so, for that reason, and that only, I write to you: now that *is* candid, but it is not quite true, for I write in the expectation of getting an answer.

"Are you astonished? You need not be. I am between four goodly walls, and fear nothing. Should you pout, what care I? unless you pout through my iron grated door, and then I will pout back again, and we will see who can pout the hardest; for that, you know, or might know, or ought to know, is a game two can play at.

"Then, if no "extraneous influence" is brought to

bear upon you, I shall have an answer; and that, in fact, is the real object of my writing. The secret is out. I would like to have you call and see me, but will not urge it. It is not a very pleasant place for a young lady to call; nor, you may think, for a young gentleman to stay. Indeed, I want to hear from you, and I want to hear the news—all the **dear** gossip—how Mr. Nichols is in jail, "poor fellow"—"too bad"—"good enough for him," &c. You have time, every qualification; we are on the right terms precisely—that is, a little friendly or so; not particular, but might be—that is—indeed I don't quite know how it is. But there is nothing to prevent you from writing as much as you please, as often as you please, and as familiarly as you please.

"Now you are sensible that under any other circumstances, I should not have been very likely to have preferred a request like this; but now, you can confer a great favor at a tolerably cheap rate, without infringing upon any rules of decorum or etiquette, or any nonsense of the kind. Furthermore, though I sue at your feet—fancy me there if you please—for this favor, yet I think I have a right to demand it. But I wont. I'll be generous. I'll not take any advantage.

"Do you remember our first walk by moonlight? I think the moon shone; if not, she ought to. Well—

before, then, since and always, I have wanted to be very friendly with you. You know I think you beautiful and charming, and all that sort of thing, only I never tell you so—'tis not my way—but of all things, I wish you were my cousin; so write me just as if you were; and I one of the cleverest fellows in all creation, which in reality I don't lack much of being—not more than I do of being, sweet girl,

Your most devoted admirer."

"P. S. I would ask you to excuse these blots, but I like to see them. An unpolluted sheet, like a faultless character, looks too d——d precise and formal. So be sure and blot yours all over."

Now what will the charming Rosalie say to all that rigmarole, I wonder? She will laugh; but will she write? I think so, and I do not often miscalculate. I made a blunder once. I laid siege to the affections of a pretty lady, and was unsuccessful—cause why? Her wedding day was set, and she was engrossed with the preparations. That was a blunder. I never made love to a bride, in the honey-moon, though!

I have just read Richelieu. If all of Bulwer's millions of readers feel towards him the same mingled feelings of admiration and gratitude that I do, I feel as if there was nothing on earth so desirable as literary fame. Horror mingles with our admiration of a victorious warrior. Blood stains his laurels—carnage placed them on his brow.

SUNDAY, JULY 7, 1839.

I was awakened this morning by the music of Frank Johnson's band. The Guards had arrived from their excursion to Detroit. Martial music of a Sunday morning is not often heard in our streets.

An United States soldier was brought in last night, in a state of unmitigated upstropulousness. He said he would be G—d d—d to h—ll if he wouldn't do as he was a mind to—ditto if he wouldn't shoot somebody; ditto if he wouldn't be as noisy as he pleased; and then he commenced breaking up the furniture of his cell. There was a fight of five minutes duration, between him and the jailer, and he was put into a cell where there was nothing to break but his own bones, and nothing but a stone floor for him to sleep upon. He "swore a prayer or two," and sunk to rest.

On the fourth of July, a lady picked some flowers, made them into a *boquet*, and sent them to me by her little girl. Sheriff Brown stood in the door and refused to let it come in. She carried it back. I never heard of such a piece of stupid tyranny. And on that day too! Never before was a prisoner denied such a present here. Never was one treated so harshly as I am. This is but a single instance. Brown acts as though he were the veriest slave of my persecutors, and sold, body and soul, to do their bidding. Charles P. Person was elected to the highly responsible office of Sheriff, by the people of Erie county. For a certain sum of money he sold the office, with its duties, emoluments and responsibilities to Brown; and when he did so, he sold the suffrages of every citizen of Erie county. It is as if the President of the United States should sell his office to the highest bidder, pocket his cash and go to Texas; and it is thus, in every thing, that our rights are trifled with and trampled on.

"Not to defend, is to relinquish," should be the motto of every republican—of every true patriot. It is not enough that our soil is free from foreign invaders, if we cherish usurpation and tyranny in our own bosom. The Laws and the Constitution are the property of the people; and they are deficient in their duty to themselves, and much more to posterity, if they tamely suffer the smallest infringement of them, especially by those who have sworn to support them, and who in violating them add *perjury to treason.* It were better for yourselves and your children, that the blood of every wilful violater of your rights should stain the pavements, than that such violation should be borne without resentment.

The man who offered, a few weeks since, if provision were made for his family, to publicly shoot down one of these men, one of the highest, though the proposition was of course rejected, was actuated by the same spirit that drove the dagger of Brutus to the heart of Cæsar.

Every freeman in Erie county, when he next goes to the ballot box, can strike at usurpation, and lawless tyranny, with more effect than with Roman steel. Every American freeman can in this way be a Brutus.

Are my shafts less felt, now that my enemies have placed me in a position where every one tells with tenfold effect? Public sympathy is always with him who acts on the defensive. But in this case, it is not sympathy alone. JUSTICE, TRUTH, LIBERTY, all are with me; and with these I cannot but triumph.

Never to the latest day of my life, shall I regret this effect of malice and crime—this illegal and tyrannical incarceration. Before, I *thought* I had the fortitude to bear adversity—now, I *know* it. And forever after, I shall date the commencement of my career from a prison, and ever be proud of it. Were heraldry the fashion, a grated cell should be the quartering of my coat of arms.

"There must be times"—says my sweetest correspondent, "when you feel gloom and despondency." *Never!*

"I was born,
"Beneath the aspect of a bright-eyed star,
"And my triumphant adamant of soul
"Is but the fixed persuasion of success."

I never even dream of failure; for well 'tis said, that

"In the Lexicon of youth, which fate reserves
"For a bright manhood, there's no such word,
"As FAIL!"

IN JAIL, JULY 8, 1839.

Read, marked and copied from Lalla Rookh—played on my violin. Music is a pretty *passer le temps*, but I either lack the genius or the patience to become an adept; yet I play for hours together, wild and strange melodies, such as are not written; and even varying, as my thoughts vary, now playful and airy—now plaintive, now sublime. It is no interruption to thought, and I can even read and play at the same time, and with the same effects.

During the whole morning there has been but one incident. I sent out my copy, which I had almost despaired of doing, so closely am I watched, and so strictly confined to my cell. The State Prison is nothing to it, and solitary confinement is esteemed one of its most terrible punishments. In some prisons it is the only one; but in New York, they flog! *She* took it, put it in her bosom, and I think will carry it safely.

The following letter is from a fellow prisoner; a man of fifty, with whom I am not allowed to converse, but we manage to correspond.

"MY DEAR SIR:—Were my mind perfectly at ease, I should feel great pleasure to take up such a subject, *currente calamo*, for my own amusement, or the gratification of the public. The vicissitudes of life, through which I have passed, present many pleasant and agreeable, but at the same time, painful and harrowing thoughts.

"I was educated for the ministry, for the service of one of the most respectable churches on earth; the

Synod of Ulster; a branch, or daughter of the Kirk of Scotland. I went through the routine of a collegiate life in a Royal University, graduated, and was licensed and ordained by some of the most eminent men of the Presbyterian order.

"I was married to the daughter of a member of the British Parliament, and started in life, with high hopes and glorious prospects. For many years I received the bounty of the British Government, and left home to follow my relatives to the wilds of America.

"There are so many diversities of opinion respecting faith in this country, that I did not connect myself with any sect, though I have preached in the first churches in the country. Several of my discourses are in print and were well received. I was solicited to unite with the Episcopal church, and have been introduced to the Bishops of New York and Quebec.

"My family are at present independent of me. My eldest son is clerk in the N. A. Fur Company, in Missouri. I became a contributor to the press, and wandered from post to pillar, without any definite object in view. Better for me had I never scribbled a line, than to have forsaken the profession for which I was educated. Age is now coming on; but I care not for that, if I once more enjoyed the pure light and liberty of heaven.

"I have studied medicine, lectured on philosophy, taught classics and edited journals. If these printers would not prosecute, I should go free. All I wanted was two or three papers, and God knows I have suffered more than all the sheets in the office were worth, in the wreck and prostration of my mind."

Such is the history of this poor man, who groans out days and nights of misery in one of these dark and filthy cells, fed on miserable garbage, and most wretchedly provided for. His crime is going into a printing office, to which he was accustomed; to get some exchange papers, to read. They found him there, and he was committed for petit larceny. A few months ago he changed umbrellas, and was proceeded against, and for lack of counsel convicted; at which no one will wonder who is acquainted with the administration of justice in Buffalo. Now he awaits in terrible suspense, a trial, which may send him to State Prison!

Ho! an incident. The ball and chain gang has returned from laboring on the streets, minus four, who filed off their chains yesterday, and to-day made their escape from the overseer.

I have received another note from my clerical friend on the other side. He says—

"DR SIR:—Another day will soon be added to the gloomy round of my slow existence. Time hangs heavily on my hands, and I would whip the lingering moments into speed.

"Rather than suffer the torments I have endured, I would rush uncalled into the realities of future scenes. By aid of the book you kindly sent me, I have been wandering, with Bulwer, through German scenery, on the banks of the Rhine; and the stories of fairies and supernatural beings recalled the innocent hours of childhood." * * *

LETTER TO MY FELLOW PRISONER.

"DEAR SIR:—To pity your misfortunes; to deeply lament the fate of one so gifted as you are, and one who might be so useful to mankind, is little; for he would be a brute who did not. I regret that you are not more of a philosopher, and submit not more cheerfully to the decrees of fate; or if you please, the dispensations of Providence: If the former, it is your interest to be content—if the latter it is your duty.

Either way, firmness is virtue. Your cell is larger than the tub of Diogenes, and no Alexander stands in your sunlight.

"Excuse me for giving advice to one so much my senior; but sir, I have had much experience crowded into a little space; and have learned to be proudly content, if not happy, under all circumstances." * * *

But what use to advise, or try to impress upon men's minds principles they cannot feel, or do not practice. Can I lessen the torture of the thumb screw by saying "bear it patiently?" The next day he writes—

"The feverish mind is still awake, and I stand giddy and fearful, trembling on the verge of a precipice. If my intentions were known, I should go unwhipped even of censure. The clang of the Court House bell, and the busy bustling of the servants of the law, only excite to a higher pitch, feelings drawn out to extreme tension."

TUESDAY, JULY 9, 1839.

Three weeks in jail to-day. Strange to say, they have passed very quickly. An almost unvaried monotony, and constant employment has made them. When my weeks are crowded with events, they seem like months; but when each day passes like the one before it, there is nothing by which to mark the lapse of time. I have been very industrious. My Journal itself would seem to be a pretty good three-week task; yet that is not half I have done.

I was thinking this morning of my enemies; and though I am not malicious, my feeling of justice is gratified by their downfall, for well they deserve it.

Nothing can strike one, acquainted with the movements of our society, more forcibly, than the fact, that no man, however popular he may have been heretofore, can attach himself to the *usurper's clique,* and become the partizan of Pratt, without losing, at once, all the hold he ever had upon the affections of the people. Barton, Taylor, Stow, Faulkner, L. F. Allen, are a few instances. No man's popularity can survive the friendship of Hiram Pratt. "His attachment is *infamy while it lasts;* and, which ever way it turns, leaves *infamy and disgrace behind it.*"

Jail, July 10, 1839.

It was a close, hot, disagreeable night. They were trying my fellow prisoners at the court house. One has got his ticket for Auburn. I pity him; but he does not grumble. The jury were eleven to one for three hours. The one then gave up, and they returned a verdict of guilty. It is strange, men cannot show better judgment, or more perseverance. My clerical friend still writes to me:

"The odium of standing as the gaze of a crowded court, I dread more than the confinement of these cheerless cells. I can pour the balm of consolation into the bosoms of others; I have sat by the bedside of struggling humanity, and seen the last sigh departing from the care-worn tenement; I have attended the funeral obsequies of men drowned and shot; I have, in the dungeon, sat beside the murderer, and join with him in prayer, previous to his launch into eternity; and now that the hand of affliction presses upon myself, I cannot profit by my own lessons." * * *

"Though one dark cloud has passed over your pathway; in the bloom of youth, and with the prospect of lengthened days before you, every thing around you, above you, and beneath you, presents music to the sense, and ravishment to the heart.

"I am glad to see that Bennett, of New York, has espoused your cause in a masterly manner. The press has more liberty in Britain and her colonies, than in this boasted land of freedom. You have begun the good work of reform; and I trust the whole rotten fabric of corruption, through your efforts here, will tumble into ruins, and moulder into decay."

This is the man they are about to send to State Prison on *suspicion* of petit larceny!

The true conservators of Liberty are the sturdy yeomanry of our country. Cities are pools of corruption.

PUBLIC MEETING AT HAMBURGH.

"At a meeting of the citizens of the town of Hamburgh, county of Erie, July 6th, 1839, the following preamble and resolutions were unanimously adopted:

"Whereas, at the late sitting of the court in and for the county of Erie, in the month of June, at the court house in the city of Buffalo, Thomas L. Nichols, Esq., editor and proprietor of a paper called the Buffalonian, was put on trial for libel; and whereas, that trial has been throughout conducted in a most extraordinary and unprecedented manner, therefore

"Resolved, That we view his conviction and incarceration in the jail of Erie county, an unwarranted outrage, not only on his rights personally, but on the rights and liberty of every American citizen.

"Resolved, That when judges on the bench stoop so low as to forget their *dignity*, by shewing partiality, they ought to be execrated by every American citizen, and consigned to eternal disgrace and infamy.

"Resolved, That we view the late proceedings of Sheriff Person, in debarring the friends of the said Thomas L. Nichols from visiting him in prison, a flagrant outrage on humanity, and only equalled by the infamous Canadian tyrant Arthur.

"Resolved, That Thomas L. Nichols, in exposing villany and rascality in high places, is entitled to the gratitude of honest men; and his enemies, to the execration of an indignant and insulted people.

"Resolved, That in Thomas L. Nichols, we see a man fearless of unprincipled enemies, and a lover of the rights of man.

"Resolved, That we owe no allegiance to moneyed aristocracy; we are not to be bought with gold, nor will we have our rights trampled upon by knaves and fools.

"Resolved, That our courts of justice in and for the county of Erie, have become corrupted by a moneyed aristocracy, and in the late trial of Thomas L. Nichols, have committed a most flagrant outrage on the feelings of every lover of liberty."

THURSDAY, July 11, 1839.

Strange things have come, and are every day coming to pass. The grand juries of Erie county, are from month to month, regularly employed in behalf of a *clique* of infamy and corruption, to put down a press, confessedly the most talented, the most independent, and the most popular, that was ever established in Buffalo. This is no vain boast. It has been for the last two years the sentiment of the public press, from one end of the country to the other; and the great mass of our independent citizens have time after time expressed the same opinion in a manner not to be mistaken.

The last grand jury but one, was so evidently *packed*, that every man cried out shame! The foreman was a man of infamous reputation. The talesmen summoned to make up the number, were, we believe, without exception, our bitter enemies; and the consequence was the finding of two paltry endictments.

A course equally infamous was taken at the last grand inquest. Early in the morning, Mr. Wilgus, ex-Alderman, employed himself in one, and probably more instances, in making inquiries of those supposed to be in our confidence, in regard to a certain article in the Buffalonian.

Strangely enough, talesmen were to be summoned to make out the proper number of grand jurors; and stranger still, this Wilgus, who had been making himself so officious, was one of the first men called!!

The result was an endictment for publishing an article I never saw or heard of, until I saw it in print; and which has been published since I have been closely confined in jail!

LETTER TO MR. G.

"My Dear Sir:—When in Detroit, nearly a year since, I had the pleasure of making your acquaintance; and to your politeness and hospitality was indebted for much of the enjoyment I found in your city. Since then I have only known you through the medium of your paper. I did anticipate paying you a visit this summer; but that, my present em-*bar*-rassing situation will prevent.

I date, as you see, from a jail, in one of the most secluded cells of which I am closely confined, for the extraordinary crime of calling a *lawyer* a *knave!* But if you have seen the report of the trial, you know all. I am "happy as a clam" and "safe as a thief in a mill." Being in jail is the true *otium cum dignitate* and the very perfection of "literary ease." Then the grates have such an air of permanence and stability about them; a right up and down look; a mathematical gravity—and when you *do* get a breath of fresh air through them it is *so* refreshing! Indeed there is nothing like it. You will never know what life, and especially editorial life, is, until you get into jail. It is in some respects better than a steamboat excursion. There is no danger of a boiler bursting, though there are some bursting chaps here; but they can't fire up, nor raise the steam. You don't fear a gale and are never sea-sick, and there is a state room for each passenger. When we lie down at night, we know pretty nearly where we shall wake up in the morning; and should exactly, but for the rats, mice and bugs.

You see I am quite too comfortably situated to think of going west this summer; and I am getting to be a very steady young man, of industrious and sedentary habits.

Our sheriff has some queer notions—I may say extraordinary ones. I was sentenced to imprisonment, and get, as near as can be, solitary confinement. My food is allowed to be brought from a friend's, provided it is of a sufficiently plain quality; the sheriff, getting only two dollars a week for what I furnish myself, is of course anxious that it should not exceed that amount in value! The other prisoners have cigars and tobacco. I don't happen to smoke or chew, but am fond of flowers; and my dear friends, the ladies, send me *boquets* almost as sweet and beautiful as themselves. They are excluded as *luxuries!*"   *   *   *

My clerical fellow prisoner was tried to-day, found guilty, and sentenced by Recorder Stow to four years imprisonment at hard labor at Auburn. Stow said he would make an example of him! And thus a brutal magistrate has consigned an unfortunate fellow creature, subject to the *same infirmity that sometimes overtakes himself;* and in intellect, education, and moral principle his superior; to a cruel, and for the offence, unheard of punishment! Such is justice in Erie county. And this same Recorder, by his own confession, on the stand, was a few months ago, an agent in suppressing charges of enormous frauds and felonies for his then employers!

LETTER TO SHERIFF PERSON.

"DEAR SIR—There is, I am sorry to inform you, but consider it my duty, much complaint among the prisoners under sentence, in regard to the extraordinary severity with which they are, just now, treated; and a great portion of it is attributed to me.

"This is, I humbly conceive, wholly unnecessary; as I am neither so unreasonable nor so malicious, as to feel aggrieved, if others are less punished than myself, or allowed far greater indulgence than I, from the *enormity* of my offence, have a right to expect. If it be true, that the other prisoners are kept in closer confinement on my account, or for fear of an accusation of partiality against yourself, I beg to assure you that such a course, so far from being agreeable to me, is highly repugnant, both to my feelings and my sense of justice.

"I know that different offences merit different degrees of punishment, and that the *heinous* crime, for which I have been so *fairly* tried and so *justly* sentenced, should be visited with all the severity it is in your power to inflict; but, Sir, permit me to say, that I do not think that every prisoner should, for that reason, be treated in the same manner; nor would I, or my friends, find fault, if all the usual indulgences were allowed to persons sentenced for the more *trivial* offences of theft, riot, assault, burglary, attempted homicide, &c. &c. On the contrary, it would give me pleasure to see others enjoying what little liberty and comfort a jail can afford, though myself deprived of it."

JULY 12, 1839.

Night. My candle is lighted, and for the first time, during this long day, I sit down to write in my Journal. In the morning, came the Buffalonian, with a bitter article on Brown, about the flowers on the Fourth. He was savage, and looked as black as a thunder cloud. It had spoiled all his smiles and affected good nature. The jailer, too, was not well pleased.

For several days there has been a falling off in my meals. To-day I found out the reason. The jailer, by order of the sheriff, stops the boy at the door, selects out every thing he fancies too good for me to eat, and sends it back, and I get the remainder. I blowed up—and called it a piece of d——d brutal tyranny. For the first time since I have been in jail I was angry. I vented it in a few refreshing curses, walked backward and forward, played a tune on my violin, and lay down and went to sleep. This is all on account of what has been published in the Buffalonian. They think to control it by severity to me. Fools! They may put me in a dungeon, with shackles on every limb, and then I would not give up the right of the freedom of the press.

John Wentworth, of the Chicago Democrat, called to see me. I knew him at Dartmouth. We were both from the Granite State, and educated in part at the same school, among her wild mountains. And we talked of old times and mutual friends.

The most beautiful smuggler in the world has brought me a basket of roses, and my cell is filled with their perfume. I gave her a kiss and a most grateful 'thank you.' She knows I love flowers, and in spite of the jailer and sheriff, brings them.

JULY 13, 1839.

So the screw has had another turn, and I am reduced to prison fare. I am the first one in this jail that ever was compelled to live upon it. My head aches—a universal depression is the consequence of a sudden deprivation of all stimulants. Tea and coffee kept up my spirits and sustained my health. In time, I suppose I shall recover the tone of my nervous system, but until I do, half my energies are gone. It is like letting out a few turns of a watch spring. All the functions of life become languid. The blood circulates slowly, the brain operates feebly.

I do not object to a simple diet, I can do without narcotic stimulants; but I would let my system down gradually. I would have the food both plentiful and palatable, and the bracing and invigorating effects of air and exercise. With these, one has little need of artificial excitements; but if ever I stood in need of the common stimulants, such as tea, coffee, and spices, it is now.

I see by my glass, that I grow pale, day by day. It is not the paleness of bad health, so much as the darkness. I am bleaching in my cell, as they bleach cellery. Every prisoner, confined for any length of time, has the same cadaverous hue. It is sometimes almost frightful to look at.

The fare itself is miserable, and yet the county pays a sufficient price. For breakfast I had a tin basin, not over bright, with a rusty iron spoon, full of soup, made by boiling refuse meat, shins of beef, etc., and thickening with flour. The meat was not over fresh, nor the soup very highly seasoned. There was a piece of tolerably good bread, and water. At noon I made interest to get a half pint of milk, in which I crumbed the remainder of my bread, and on that I dined. At supper time, round came the old tin basin, with mush—a pudding of Indian meal and water—and with it some unpalatable, and thinly diluted molasses. No coffee—no tea—nothing but what I have mentioned. I do not believe there is a prison in the country where the diet comes so near starvation.

JULY 14, 1839.

More myself again. I try to invigorate myself by exercise, but am confined too closely; and in my cell, there is not room even to swing my arms about. The air too, is not fit for human beings to breathe. Yet I stand it bravely. Every day has some incident or adventure. The conversation of the prisoners is not wholly destitute of amusement, though generally of the very lowest species of flash blackguardism.

Day before yesterday, a "gentleman," who has been confined for some time on charge of theft, was discharged for want of evidence. Yesterday he visited us, dressed in a new suit of clothes, which he had *realized* that morning. In the evening he was married to a very pretty girl, and before two o'clock this morning, was again committed to jail, on charge of bigamy, it having appeared to the satisfaction of the magistrate that he has six living wives. This was doing a pretty stroke of business. His wife—the new one—did not like it. She came to the jail, but was refused admission; but this morning her father brought her here, and she is at his request now closely confined up stairs; and the new bride and bridegroom are not allowed to see each other.

I have had a visit from a beautiful lady. She came with a friend of mine, and he introduced her to the jailer as his wife, but I knew very well she was not. I tried to think who she was, or where I had seen her, though her's is not a face or form to forget. Tall, graceful, with brilliant complexion, full black eyes and raven hair, she is one to live long in a man's memory; still I could not remember her. I began to think I was growing confused, and my mind was suffering unconsciously. I gazed at her in evident admiration—I gave her two of my most beautiful flowers. She received them gracefully. I looked in the glass, and asked if I had grown pale. "I cannot tell" said she, "for I never saw you before!"

Never!—and I looked at her again. I took down

my violin, and thumbed an air. My friend sung. We were talking together. She had turned her head away, and appeared absorbed with the flowers. I heard a sob—and she burst into tears. I knew not what to say or think. They took their leave, and as she left, she turned back to say farewell. Her bosom heaved with emotion, she could not speak, her tears burst forth afresh, and she signed me a silent farewell. As they passed through the yard, she held the flowers in her delicate hands, and her tearful eyes were still turned towards my cell. Who she may be, or what is her name, I have yet to find out; but it is all very strange.

LETTER TO MIRANDA.

"I am luxuriating upon the sweet aud beautiful flowers you sent me. How lovely they look! and yet, I would give more to see you for one half hour than for all the roses that ever bloomed in the vale of Cashmere. One glance at your face, beautiful with every kindly emotion, and the soft tones of your voice for a moment, would be better than all the flowers that bloom, much as I love them.

"My dear girl, I am most grateful—tears start into my eyes as I write to you. When you came into the prison, I was almost asleep. I heard the soft tones of your voice, and started up as from a dream, broken with pleasant music. I sprang up—my heart beat—Miranda, I am not weak, but I am in a prison. There is not one here with whom I have one feeling in common. I have no one to love—no loved one near me. Father, mother, friends, are far away. My dear sister, whom I love as my soul, is not here. I am glad she is not, for they would not allow her to see me. Think me not weak then, if your kindness affects me, even to tears. I do not often shed them. I cannot be coerced, nor frightened by threats. I scorn to bow to insolence or tyranny; but love and kindness melt me at once.

"I am glad to see you looking so well. You never looked so beautiful. I was thinking of the verses of Moore—

"Oh! had we some bright little isle of our own,
In a blue summer ocean, far off and alone."

There all by ourselves, how sweetly might pass the golden hours—but such things are not, and we must take the harsh, rough world as we find it, and joyously make the best of it.

"The perfume of those flowers fill my cell, and every breath I inhale reminds me of her to whose love I owe them. For your sake, sweet, excellent, heroic girl, I would I had boundless wealth and a monarch's power. You should be happy—happy as you deserve; if all that could charm the senses could make you so. Do not mistake me. When I say this, it is with single reference to your own deserts, and not to my feelings. The romance of life, with me is over. My passions are schooled—reason holds her empire, and even you, could not move me from my purpose. I would do any thing to oblige you, consistent with honor and duty. To violate those, you would never in your heart desire me. You are too noble—too sensible—too good."

MONDAY, July 15, 1839.

My headache is over, but I do not feel like writing. I can scarcely rouse myself to the least mental exertion. I shall have to resort to opium or brandy, and I like neither. Tobacco I will not use. Opium nauseates me. Brandy is not the right sort of excitement. A preparation of morphia would do, with a vegetable acid to correct it. Well, 'twill soon be over.

Yes, all the bright summer is passing away;
  Soon the bleak winds of Autum will round us be moaning;
I count every week, I number each day,
  Yet think not the captive with misery groaning.

I look up to the high vault of heaven at eve—
  I can see a small piece of the sky from my cell,
So little indeed, it you well may believe,
  Like a far glimpse of heaven to the tortured in hell.

Yes, hell—for this prison's a hell upon earth;
  There is "weeping, and wailing, and gnashing of teeth;"
There are curses and groans, diabolical mirth,
  And a set of poor devils lie down underneath.

Each one has a cannon ball chained to his leg,
  Each is filthy and ragged, and haggard and pale;
The constables swore they had known them to beg,
  So Barton has sent them for six months to jail.

Tuesday, July 16, 1839.

Another week. I have been copying my bill of exceptions, for the Supreme Court, whose decision I shall wait most anxiously. At last I have a letter from Rosalie. It was written very soon after mine, but just now received.

"I *was* fearful," she writes, "that the petty tyranny of those in whose power for the present you are placed, would weigh upon your mind and make you, at least, unhappy. It has not, and it must not. Remember that many of the great and good of earth, have, like you, been

'Condemned to chains unholy;'

and that it has been one means of gaining for them a deathless fame. May it be so with you.

"If I have gained *your* friendship, I am thankful and proud to have done so. You want I should tell you all the 'dear gossip.' Well, then, 'every body' says that 'it is a shame Mr. Nichols is in prison,' and that 'such things are not to be borne,' and that they 'are going to do something.' What, they do not know. When they threatened putting you on the ball and chain gang, a lady told me that were they to do it, she would, with her own fair fingers, undo the fetters. You must not distrust your friends. They are true."

And thus writes Rosalie, one of the most beautiful, high souled girls that ever a young poet wrote sonnets to; yet she is scarcely in her teens. I don't see how a man of sense can avoid loving such girls.

LETTER TO ROSALIE.

"Jail, July 16.

"My Dear Friend:—You *are* a good, and a charming correspondent. Yours, of the 7th, I had almost ceased to expect; but not quite, for I thought I knew you.

"I am still in good spirits—still cheerful—sometimes I am as gay as you ever saw me. You have not *gained* my friendship, you had it, from the first moment I saw you. I cannot help loving such as you; I cannot avoid being the friend of the lovely and the good. I am yours; and now, more than ever; and had I another sister to choose, of all the world, it should be you. That's frank. I know not what alteration two years and a half may have made in my own sister, but when I saw her last, I thought her beautiful; but, better than that, she was ever amiable, kind and affectionate, the soul of gayety and good nature, yet full of feeling and spirit. Oh! I have seen her dark eyes flash so beautifully. There was something sublime in her momentary passion. I loved her as brother loves sister, and the world has no such love beside. Indeed she was the light and joy of my existence.

"I am very much obliged to my friends for their sympathy, good wishes, etc.; and who could be the lady who would sprain her delicate fingers in tugging at my shackles, provided I wore them? The task were more befitting a son of Vulcan, than a rival of Venus.

"Why restrict yourself to one page? Is there more harm in a long letter than a short one? No. It is those little, short, three-cornered yes and no P. S. letters that do all the mischief. Who ever knew a long letter or a long story to have any mischief in it? You may write me sixteen pages, nor then need your excellent aunt "look lectures." I don't think they look agreeable, and she is far too good looking a lady to spoil her features in that absurd way.

"I read more than for a long time I have had opportunity. I sing, write and fiddle; but nothing makes time pass so quickly as writing and reading letters. I manage to scribble rhymes too, which is the strangest phenomenon of my imprisonment. I have always contended that I was no poet, which I think will not be disputed; but what is stranger, I have uniformly refused to write verses, even in ladies' albums, when beseeched most beseechingly; but now, rhymes come uncalled for, and the muses, who never favored me before, seem at last to have taken pity on me. The following lines I wrote the other day, to a young lady, almost as beautiful as yourself, and certainly one of the very prettiest in Buffalo."

SUNSET—TO ———

The burning sun in splendor set—
　The clouds of purple and of gold
Around him glowed; and never yet
　Did earth or heaven a scene unfold,
Of radiant beauty, fair and bright,
More glorious than gleam'd upon my raptured sight.

So thought I, till one blessed day
　My eyes looked in the depths of thine,
Which shot from thy bright soul a ray
　Of sparkling mind! of light divine!
Then I confessed the splendors of that night
Ill matched thy glowing cheeks, and eyes of heavenly light.

WEDNESDAY, July 17, 1839.

A girl, modest and pretty looking, but whom I never saw before, came to see me. I wonder who she could be. She had as much of a waiting maid look, as a yankee ever has, and with a roguish devil lurking in her blue eye, seemed overjoyed to see me, sprang forward, and I thought was about to embrace me; but she only shook me warmly by the hand, leaving in it a letter. It was managed most adroitly, and we were good friends in a moment. Pretty soon she left me, looking drolly at the jailer who in the exercise of his duty had heard every word and watched every motion; and bidding me a playful "good bye," both vanished, leaving me to read my

LETTER FROM JULIA.

"My Dear Friend:—Do you think I could let one week pass, without seeing you, if to see you were possible? Indeed I could not. To pass an hour with you is one of my greatest pleasures—I may add, the only pleasure. Last week I went to the jail to make you a call; I knocked; in a moment the door was opened, and I expected to see you. Imagine what were my feelings, when I was denied permission. I could not believe it. To make sure, I asked again, but was very plainly given to understand that I could not see you!

"Oh! how different were my feelings, when returning from that gloomy, dreadful place, from the delightful anticipations I felt when going to it. I looked up at your window as I was passing, in hopes of seeing you through its gratings—even that would have been some consolation; but my eyes were dim; I am not sure I could have seen you had you been there. Little Jane, my niece, and one of your warmest friends, accompanied me, and was as much disappointed as I was. Afterward she went alone, but even that little child was refused admittance. She came weeping home, her little heart ready to break with their inhumanity.

* * * * * *

"They are trying, if possible, to stop your press; and the reason given by your enemies for your close confinement, is, that you may not throw copy out of the window. It is the opinion of many that they will keep you in jail for a year or longer. Impossible!— but what can they not do?

"Last evening I walked by your prison. Your cell was lighted, and I could see you through the grates. You were either reading or writing. I stood some moments, looking at you, and wishing I could speak only one word to you. Your little friend, Jane, was with me. She talks of you incessantly. She was glad to see you, but most sorry to see you there. She kissed her little hand, and said "good night;" but you could not hear her. It was a lovely night, and sad and melancholly as I felt, the conversation of my young companion soothed my feelings—for she talked of you, and I love her more than ever for being your friend.

"P. S. Tuesday night. I have just returned from my usual walk. I have been looking at you. You were standing up—I think, looking in the glass. Imagine you see me before your window to-morrow night at half past eight. Keep the light close to you; I can see much plainer; and hold it in your hand, that I may know you are thinking of me."

The fair and gentle Julia is not the only unseen visiter I have, after twilight. The jailer says there are ladies—sometimes alone, sometimes accompanied by gentlemen, in the jail yard, almost every pleasant evening; and I often hear low sweet voices, like music, around me, as if the hovering spirits were conversing; and sometimes I see the gleam of a white dress in the fading twilight. Some come from curiosity, probably most; but some I am sure from sympathy and friendship. Julia is not the only one who has been excluded, nor the only lady. One of my warmest friends, and one to whom I am under many obligations, came to see me with her daughter, a fairy creature of eleven summers, and both were refused. The latter came afterwards; she even made two trials, but could not gain admittance. She begged the jailer to take me a cake, which he dared not do. Such is the brutal tyranny of the contemptible under sheriff.

> I know not whether he's more knave or fool;
> Himself a tyrant; or a tyrant's tool!

But I think a little of both. He gloats over every form of human misery, and subsists on the starvation of his fellow beings.

FRIDAY, JULY 19, 1839.

All are not refused, for to-day I had a visit from Mrs. P. of the theatre. I was very glad to see her, for she is a woman of genius and sensibility, and not afraid either to speak her mind or to visit a friend in misfortune. She would be an honor to any station.

Last night, by a most mysterious process, savoring strongly of magic, a large cake and a bottle of delicious wine found its way into my cell. It was a mysterious affair. Did the walls open to admit them, or was it only the flinty heart of the tall jailer. There must have been witchcraft, and at one moment I saw the sparkle of a most bewitching eye, like a diamond in the dark, and I caught, I am sure, the bright gleam of a petticoat. It must have been a witch, and the cake and wine came in by incantation; so I canted the bottle over my silver goblet, and decanted a portion of its delicious contents.

Wonders will never cease. To-day I had three distinguished visiters. The Rt. Hon. Fred. Emmons, Major Benjamin Holt, and John O'Brien, Esq., late High Sheriff. The Rt. Hon. Fred. Emmons, gave me a circumstantial account of his interview, with the Hon. Henry Clay, whom he familiarly called Hank, at General Burt's party, where, at the head of a large number of highly respectable citizens, accompanied by a fife and drum, they marched in at the front door, drowned the music of the cotillion band, put a stop to the dancing, made the house totter with three cheers for Henry Clay, and drank up the liquor. A conversation ensued between Fred and Hank, on politics and matters and things in general, and both displayed their eloquence to great advantage. Fred thinks it was a "great lick."

What a mine of character is Buffalo! No place in the world has more originality. Much like it is the whole country bordering on the great lakes. I am getting together material, which will last me a life time. Even in jail, I have an opportunity for studying character, I never had before. There is a whole jailer, a sheriff, and officers. There are counterfeiters, burglars, robbers, and rowdies. A wild Irishman, and wild Indians, a priest, a schoolmaster, a shingle maker, a bigamist, and a cattle stealer from Yorkshire, gamblers, petit larcenists, and vagrants, poor debtors, and poor devils, black, white and copper colored.

What! more letters?—yes—here is one from Wm. Lyon Mackenzie, dated,

"Jail of Monroe County, July 6.

"DEAR SIR:—When we last met, I believe neither of us expected to congratulate each other through the bars of a penitentiary; but so it is. We are both locked up, and I must own you bear it more philosophically than I, irritating in the highest degree, as the usage you meet with would be to any man. But my age is double yours. Youth looks forward to victory, buoyant with hope; age looks back to the past, fearful that it is but the image of the future!"

* * * * * *

"'Tis well for you that you are unmarried. I have up-hill work in this country, that's a fact! The path to heaven is represented as rugged—so have I found the path of honest patriotism.

"I never heard of confinement like yours under such circumstances; but I should think it would rouse the better feelings of your fellow citizens in your behalf. I hope it will do so.

Truly Yours."

Oh! delicious mush and molasses! Oh! bone soup, extatic! The jailer has got angry at the wild Irishman, and swears by Jupiter, Mars, and Vulcan especially, as well as two or three of the goddesses, that he will put him in irons. Patrick will be of no more use to himself.

A letter from Brother Ned. He says—"I was not much surprised at the event, (my imprisonment) for I had not the most remote idea of your final triumph, even though you had published nothing but truth; and I have never doubted that you were convinced of the corruption of your enemies, and I supposed you were correct in your opinions, but expected that you would be overpowered by this very corruption." What a sensible brother!

He writes from Sherbrooke, Lower Canada, and says,—"Last winter your weekly was sent regularly, and read by almost the whole village; and while they used to dislike its radicalism, they would always read it, and often inquire of the person to whom they were sent if he had any more of *'those mad papers.'* "

So it has been, every where. No newspaper in this country was so eagerly read—none more widely circulated.

I flatter myself that the following is a *perfect* specimen of Album Poetry. It ought always to be written on a mush and molasses diet—e. g.

TO L———.

Fair girl, enchantment breathes around
    Thy form of glowing grace,
And witchery, that my heart hath bound,
    Lurks in that lovely face.

I've gazed upon thy cheek's rich glow,
    Thy brow of spotless white,
Thy teeth of pearl, thy neck of snow,
    Thine eyes of heavenly light;

Yet less I prize thy beauties rare,
    Less round my heart they're twined,
Than those far richer treasures are,
    The beauties of thy mind.

SATURDAY, July 20, 1839.

They are putting the shackles on the prisoners who have been sentenced to Auburn. Among the rest, is my correspondent. He wanted me to get him some prussic acid. Not knowing where it could be procured I begged he would excuse me. If he insisted upon giving up the ghost, I couldn't help it, and would be the last one to interfere with his reserved rights, but he must excuse my rendering him any assistance in the case. The laws are very tyrannical, and public opinion sensitive; and I wonder how he could ask me to expose myself. He might almost as well ask me to lend him money. Besides, I wanted him to show more *grit*. It was out of character for a man like him to repine, and talk of poison. Were it a hanging matter, he might choose between a halter and poison; but a State Prison is a different case. In short, I wouldn't get the prussic acid, and so spoiled what might have been a bit of tragedy.

My fair unknown, my sympathetic black eyed beauty, called to-day. She pretended to the jailer she only wanted to look round the jail. He thought he knew better. To make it appear so, she started to walk round the other side. Mr. Jailer told her there was no one there she wished to see! Being of the same opinion, she altered her mind and came to my cell. She sat and talked half an hour, and told me her story, which was very romantic; and at parting shook hands and burst into tears: Oh! I threw myself on the bed, and tried to imagine what should produce such an exhibition of exquisite sensibility—then got up and looked in the glass. 'Tis not an ugly face, and looks now more "pale and interesting" than usual: but there is nothing killing or heart breaking about it.

Received a most tender and beautiful letter from Julia, which I answered, and then wrote one to my good father.

Sunday Night.

I don't know that it is strange I should rather write letters, than to merely scribble my "loose thoughts" in this book, which the world is never to see, and perhaps not even my most intimate friends—yet I shall keep it as long as I live. Is there any thing I should be ashamed of? I think not. So I wrote a letter to Miranda, full of love and passionate nonsense.

Richardson makes Sir Charles Grandison in love with two accomplished and beautiful ladies at the same time. Now if a man can love two, why not six, and so on, *ad infinitum?* Admit it, and King Solomon, when he promised to "love and cherish" all his three hundred wives, and kept seven hundred mistresses beside, did not commit a very great absurdity. Man's affections are wonderfully expansive. *Apropos*—Sampson went, with the rest, to Auburn five years, for bigamy.

Winchell, the celebrated imitator and ventriloquist, whose drolleries have delighted all who have listened to his personations, has composed a negro song, on my imprisonment. He sung it for several nights at the garden, and never without a double or treble *encore.* Saturday night, on the occasion of Mrs. Pierce's benefit, he sung it at the theatre; and the largest and most fashionable audience of the season *encored* it four times. Such is public sentiment. Following are some verses of the song; which, in literary merit, is at least *equal* to the best of its class.

SCIENCE JACK.

When walking in the fields one day, I heard a piteous wail;
It seemed to cry along de sky, "Poor Nichols is in jail!"
    Chorus.—Oh! will you, will you, white man,
        Will you, will you, white man, let him go?

Den an Eagle flew right o'er my head, and lit upon a rail;
I axed him what's de news? he said
   Spoken—"Look yeh, Nigger; don't you know dat Nichols is in jail."
               Oh! will you, &c.

"Now listen, Science Jack," said he, den he began to sing;
"He's talents bright, and de quill dat he writes was plucked from an eagle's wing."
               Oh! will you, &c.

"Now his spirit soars on eagle's wings, he's de heart ob a lion bold;
Aldo dey may chain his body down, yet his soul can't be controlled."
               Oh! will you, &c.

Now I axed dis bird what I should do; he answered wid a shout,
"Just go right back to Buffalo, and try for to sing him out."
               Oh! will you, &c.

"Now de ladies fair are de first dat dare to speak for de oppressed,
And de gentleman too will support you true, if you but do your best."
               Oh! will you, &c.

I shook his claw—we parted, he soon flew out ob sight;
I gazed in de air, not a speck was dere, he'd melted into light.
               Oh! will you, &c.

Now dey broke into his office fus, dey tore his press all flat;
Dey blacked demselves like darkies, but dey got well paid for dat.
               Oh! will you, &c.

Dey tried dem in de court house, dey too was held to bail,
Dey was fined pretty high, but 'twas all in my eye, for dey was not sent to jail.
               Oh! will you, &c.

Dey took him for a libel, dey've crammed him into a cell,
Dey'll keep him dare as long as dey can, kase he can write so well.
        Oh! will you, &c.

Now dere's some folks dey got money, and dere's some folks dey got none—
When de rich man treads on de poor man's neck, den our liberty is done.
        Oh! will you, &c.

This was sung, published in the Buffalonian, and hawked on handbills.

        WEDNESDAY NIGHT, July 24.

Last night I got some cake, cheese and raisins. I ate some, and this morning quoted Shakspeare most feelingly.

    "Oh! I have passed a miserable night;"

and such is the altered tone of my digestive system, from the horrid jail diet, that I have been sick all day from dyspepsia. Read Swift and Dr. Johnson.

THURSDAY, July 25.

Still weak, languid and indolent. I cannot write. I can scarcely read. All the morning I was in a dreamy stupefaction.

Darrow says I have got an up-hill business: that they have the power, and are determined to push it as hard as possible. We shall see. It is strange that in a republic, I am submitting daily to the most odious despotism; with the majority in my favor, the minority still tyrannizes over and oppresses me; with the good feelings of four fifths of our population on my side, I am beyond its beneficial influence. In some communities, the tyrants would have *felt*, ere this, the power of public opinion.

LETTER FROM ROSALIE.

"It was not repentance nor forgetfulness that detained my letter. I sent it the first opportunity. You say you are still in good spirits. Need I tell you how glad I am to hear it? Your enemies may confine the body, but they are all powerless to fetter the mind. Let them deny you every thing they can, and you will still have your own beautiful thoughts; still have the proud consciousness that you have done right; and that for nobly and chivalrously defending the weak against the oppression of the strong, you have been made to feel every species of tyranny their craven spirits could invent. Some, no doubt, rejoice at every new indignity heaped upon you, but are they not those whose approval you would feel degraded in receiving?

"I had a strange dream the other night, and as you played a conspicuous part in it, I shall send it. I thought there was a 'hurrying to and fro,' as if some strange and wild excitement had seized upon our sober citizens. I heard the clash of arms, the shout of victory, the triumphant huzza, the loud and joyous acclamations of happy hearts. Right merrily it sounded. Then I saw *you*, surrounded by a crowd of congratulating friends, whose lips spake, and whose eyes beamed joy at the sight of you, the defender of their rights. I was awakened with 'breakfast ready.'

" 'Alas that dreams are only dreams!' "

*   *   *   *   *   *

Jail, Friday, July 26, 1839.

The air is hot—hot as the Sirocco. It is stifling. The candle flares and melts in it. The insects, of which the atmosphere is full, seem to buzz about with new activity, while the crawling creatures of this infernal den have all come forth from their hiding places. I gasp—gasp. Oh! 'tis rare, this!

There is a groan, and there a curse. Heavens, what energy! In the place below, they may have louder ones, but scarcely deeper. In truth, they are not much to be blamed; and I wonder how the poor fellows bear it so well. Only think—shut out from the blessed light of Heaven, the fresh breath of the Almighty, the glorious scenes of nature, from friends, society, all that makes life dear; and shut up in a place like this! What wonder that they groan and curse?

There seems to be peculiar ingenuity in the tortures of this place. I have read over the statutes, and some of the provisions seem to be perfectly gratuitous. Such is the exclusion of fruit and flowers. The sheriff of Erie county is wiser than the Almighty, who dispenses his blessings alike to the good and evil. Even the beautiful *boquet* of "Crown Imperials," could not get in at the door, but by some magic walked in at the window.

Then there is a colony of magnificent rats, of the largest dimensions, kept at the expense of the county; unless, indeed, they belong to the private establishment of the sheriff; to worry the prisoners, eat up their provisions, and gnaw their noses in their helpless hours of sleep.

Next come the bed-bugs, of which there is an immense and constantly increasing population. This is as far as it is expedient to go in this matter, but we might descend several degrees, the county tormentors growing

"Small by degrees and beautifully less."

So much for the animal tribe. These, by aid of poisons, perfumes and fresh linen, one may be partially rid of; but these cannot relieve one from profanity, blackguardism, and the coarse ebullitions of constitutional loaferism. But these may be borne. Divine philosophy conquers all; and strange as it may seem, even here, "a sound mind in a sound body" may make a man happy.

My cell is the one occupied for almost two years by Benjamin Rathbun. I well remember the feelings with which I first saw it; and the other day I turned back to the description I then gave of my first impression of my present "location." It was in manner following, to wit:

"I knocked at the prison door. The heavy bolts were drawn—the iron door grated harshly on its hinges, and I passed up the narrow staircase and along the dark passages. Groans and execrations, and wild laughter broke from the grated cells. I came to the last—the ponderous padlock was removed—the iron door thrown open, and I stood in the presence of the man whom I had learned to love, from the united testimony of every man who was ever in his employ; nay, from the children of want and wretchedness who had lost their benefactor. He was seated in a chair, the only one his cell contained, at the head of a cot bedstead. He received me politely, apologised good humoredly for the poorness of his accommodations, and offered me a seat on his bed. The cell may be three and a half or four feet wide by eight long. I sat on the cot bedstead, my back against one wall and my feet touching the other. There is just space enough beside the bed for a chair, and at the foot was a small wash stand. At first I could not distinguish him, it was so dark. The cell has no window, and the light comes through two sets of iron gratings. In cloudy weather it is too dark to read or write.

Here in this strong cell, with its iron door locked, deprived of liberty, of friends—deprived even of the blessed light of Heaven, in solitude, in darkness, with no sounds but the curses and brutal merriment of the wretched beings around him; he stays day after day, month after month, &c. &c."

Thus I wrote of another, long before I ever anticipated occupying the same place as a reward for the sympathy I exprsssed for him.

LETTER TO ROSALIE.

"My Charming Friend:—I have no business, no company, no excuse—nothing but the yawning dullness of this sleepy place to hinder me from writing to you. I know not that my letters please you, but yours come like a ray of blessed sunlight into a gloomy cavern—like a cool zephyr, "wafted o'er beds of violets" in a sultry day—like a clear, sparkling spring, in a desert—like a herald of happiness to the lonely; and give me such joy as you beings of sunlight and freedom cannot know.

"I should have answered yours last night as soon as I received it; but I wanted to read it over, to muse upon it, "to sleep, perchance to dream;" for sometimes I do have beautiful and glorious dreams; but alas! they fade at dawn of day with all of night's lights and shadows—they go out like the stars, and are forgotten.

"Your dream—I think 'twas but fancy's picture of a thought—perhaps a wish fulfilled. It is strange, but you are the third or fourth lady who has written me that I have been the subject of her dreams. Should I not be proud of inspiring so many fair ones' "night thoughts?" I will have yours a happy omen; not that I hope for its accomplishment; but because it proves that one of the fairest and dearest of my friends does not forget me. I do not allow myself to think of freedom here. It will be time enough, when I can enjoy it.

"My sister would *love* you; and if she knew that you were my friend—that you wrote me kind letters to cheer the gloom of my prison, she would adore you. Form not too high an opinion of her personal beauty. Judge it not by your own; but imagine, that with more perfect features, a softer contour, fairer complexion, with no care-worn wrinkles, a richer color and a finer eye, she resembles me, and you have her picture. My brother Ned, in his last letter, calls her "the brightest and best, the loveliest girl that ever cheered a parson's fireside;" but that too, is a brother's eulogy—to a brother, though.

"I am a worse egotist than ever. I wish you were half as much of one. Years ago I read Helen, and admired it very much; but now have quite forgotten all but the impression it produced. And you have 'supped full of horrors' on the scenes of that bloody revolution. How that gay licentious capital, reeking with blood, must have looked in the eye of Heaven! Where were the thunders of Almighty wrath? The hearts of guilty and innocent, old and young, male and female, helped to swell the tide of blood.

"You need not hurry about 'growing steady,' I doat on romps. It is rather the most amiable propensity—romping is—that young ladies are possessed of. They ought to indulge it as long as possible; matrimony will bring a cure fast enough, though I have heard of married romps.

"I shall be very happy to see you at my 'boarding house.' I do not mistake your motives, and shall ever be grateful for your kindness. For your amiability, your frankness, and the unaffected goodness of your heart, which prompted you to amuse and enliven the weary hours of a prisoner, I shall ever esteem you, and ever be your friend."

A man from Ohio came to jail to-day, sentenced by Barton. Crime—giving an Indian sixpence to jump off one of the canal bridges. Committed under the riot act!

A good looking sailor brought in, very drunk. "Jack's on–hic–a spree–hic;" and down he fell on the pavement. He was disarmed of a big jack-knife, with the spring broken, and a pistol without any lock. There are locks enough here.

Lawyer called—wanted to ask me a question in private—not allowed. Jailer threatened to put all the prisoners in shackles—thought he spake *iron*-ically.

Patrick likes the living very well, but complains of the bed-bugs. He has been speculating in the clothing line. Those who were sentenced to state prison, sell all their good clothes, and spend the money on the way.

Got a very beautiful, passionate, and delicious letter from Miranda, to which I replied immediately, at length; and as it contains a little auto-biography never before written, I shall copy it into this my Journal. Hem!

LETTER TO MIRANDA.

"I have no visiters—no ladies. It is strange that a young lady of your good sense will write and speak almost pettishly upon that subject. You tell me of your walks, your social enjoyments; and yet upon the supposition, that some lady calls and spends an hour with me sometimes, you write as if you were jealous of me. Had you not written me a long and very beautiful letter, I would censure you. Can I never convince you how very foolish it is to be jealous?

I have no delicious moonlight walks to tell you of. My life is one of almost unchanging monotony. The greatest event is when I get a letter; and I do not mean to flatter you when I say that none affect me so much or give me so much pleasure as yours. You are, to me, a marvel and a mystery. It is as if in some dark place, I had found a bright and lovely gem, and was enraptured with its beauty—as if on the trackless and sterile desert, I had found one lonely flower, and hung over its odor—as if in a waste of ruins, I had discovered some masterpiece of art, and was silently and admiringly contemplating its perfections. You, Miranda, are that gem, that flower, that statue.

"How fresh and beautiful is your picture of that

scene by the lake. I shall never forget it—nor those pure and holy thoughts, that rose, spirit-winged, to Heaven. It was a calm and happy hour, such as you find but few of in this world; and if your thoughts dwelt for a moment on the dark cell, where bars of iron guard me, the contrast increased rather than diminished your pleasure. Such is the natural tendency of sympathetic emotions.

"Oh! how beautiful is the earth, with its green fertility and fresh loveliness—its quiet nooks, and its vast wilds and dreary solitudes. Earth has many bright and glorious scenes; and among mankind there are those who deserve to be gods for their nobleness. I have known some—alas! a very few, and even these had their foibles.

"You say you like love stories. Shall I tell you some of my amours? My first *affaire de cœur* was when I was about ten years old. Ellen was three years older. We went to the same school, corresponded, and all that. She was one of the most perfectly beautiful blonds I ever saw. I kept her letters a long time, but lost or destroyed them. Ellen moved away. I have never seen her since, but if I understand the passion, I loved her very sincerely.

"My next flame was Emily. She was a beauty too, but of a different style from Ellen. I had grown older and more romantic, and my passion was now of a much loftier character; for I was now in my twelfth year. Emily was the daughter of a widow lady of refined taste and amiable character. I loved this excellent lady, but I adored her eldest daughter. She had the form of a sylph—raven ringlets floated over a neck of alabaster—her complexion had more of the lily than the rose, and her eyes were black, and the most expressive I had ever looked into; and whole days did I spend in that employment, and listening to her charming voice. Those were my days of romance. I wandered on the banks of the river, or among the rocks and dark woods. I grew pale, melancholy and *Werterish*. 'I never told my love,' and my 'damask cheek' suffered severely. I got over it, though.

"It was more than a year before I was seriously in love again, for I count my little flirtations nothing.

"Mary was something of the same style of beauty, though of a more voluptuous cast. She like the others was several years my senior; for when boys fall in love, it is always with those who are older than themselves. I walked, read, sung and talked with her; I pressed her soft hand to my lips, and vowed I loved one glance of her eye better than life.

"At fourteen I saw Eugenia. She was beautiful as a wild rose, and the belle of our village. Almost every evening—summer evenings like these, I used to sit with her in her little *boudoir*, in a rocking-chair large enough to hold us both, when she sat in my lap; and there for hours together, we would sit and talk and sing; my arm encircled her waist; hers was about my neck. The grouping was charming.

'Lip to lip, and breast to breast.'

It was Eugenia who taught me to kiss scientifically, for she was an adept. Previous to that, I had been a bungler in the matter. There is as much difference in people in kissing as in dancing, drawing, or any thing which requires both taste and skill. But I am writing to one who might grace a professorship of this polite accomplishment.

"I have skipped one; but I will not describe her. It was a passion as violent as short lived; and though the image of the enchanting rustic is graven on my memory, I cannot recall her name.

"Eliza and I had a sort of sentimental friendship, at times somewhat ardent, but very disinterested; and for two years I spent much of my leisure in her society.

"I had got to be seventeen. I supposed the romance of my life over; but one day a little fairy caught my heart while my philosophy was napping. Mark the change. She was two years younger than I, and my passion was of an altered character. I went regularly through the different stages of the complaint; the inflammatory, the nervous, the heroic, poetic, and the melancholic. Matrimony, of course, was not to be thought of; so for the next best cure I tried absence.

"There—I shall tell you no more. You have the history of my heart, a portion of it, up to my eighteenth year. If you wish it, at some other time I will bring it up to date. What I have told you is true, and not more strange than all my early life. Love was always a part of my being. I was the most remarkable enthusiast you ever saw; but I got bravely over it. Ask for no more long letters."

WEDNESDAY, July 31, 1839.

On Monday, the city was the scene of the greatest excitement I ever knew in Buffalo. Capt. Appleby was accused of an outrage upon a girl, on board the Constitution. The conduct of Justice Barton, raised a feeling of indignation against both him and Appleby.

The latter was committed to jail to await a requisition from the Governor of Ohio, and Barton mobbed, and compelled to resign his office. So far good. Monday night, some thousands of people surrounded the jail, and cheered me. I could not think what it could be about. Again and again, the welkin rung with hurras. The sheriff and officers were trying to preserve order. The mob insisted upon seeing me at the window. The sheriff refused to open the door of my cell, nor would he, until afraid that the jail would be torn down. I made a very short speech, and they cheered me and dispersed.

Appleby has always treated me politely. I have sailed with him, and eaten at the same table on shore. He offered me a state room and free passage west, the evening before my sentence. I cannot think him guilty of the crime with which he is charged, and have treated him, and shall treat him accordingly. His wife comes to see him every day.

LETTER FROM MY SISTER.

"D——y Vt. July 21, 1839.

"My Dear Brother:—Would a letter from me do you any good? or need I asssure you of a sister's remembrance and love? I need not describe our feelings. Already have you imagined them. Yet our grief is nothing, compared with what it would have been had your imprisonment been caused by crime. No—the feeling that you are innocent, and that you have the consciousness of integrity to sustain you, is a great relief.

"Gladly, my dear brother, would I fly to you—gladly would I share with you your lonely cell, if circumstances did not make it impossible. I thought seriously of going, and father was anxious I should; but a letter from Miss H. has changed my destination to the South. * * * * * *

"After all, how *do* you like being deprived of liberty? I wish I could be with you. It seems to me that a prison would not be dreary with you. Is it not a blessed thing that man cannot chain the soul—that he has no power to shackle memory, imagination and reason—that though he deprives you of the presents and kind attentions of friends, the luxuries and comforts of life, of sounds pleasant to the ear, and sights charming to the eye, he cannot take away those resources within, which after all, are the real and most substantial springs of happiness—that he cannot take away the consciousness of innocence, without which, no one can be happy, and possessing which no one can be miserable. Happy is it for us both, that we do not depend entirely upon outward circumstances for pleasure. If you cannot see your friends, you can love them still. Your *affections* are not chained.

"You have books for your companions. They are friends who are never jealous, envious or unkind—who never change with the changes of fortune, but still cheer, amuse, and instruct us in every vicissitude of life; and even should they take away your books, you could think.

"Father would come and see you, but it is not possible for him to leave home for so long a journey. Mother feels as if it were dreadful to have to go to prison, and all that." * * * *

SATURDAY, August 3, 1839.

My lovely friend Rosalie came to see me, and was refused admittance. Go on! heap it up! I bide my time. The dear enthusiast writes—

"I *know* you will finally triumph. The tide of public opinion sweeps onward like a resistless flood, bearing, to the guilty clique, disgrace and destruction. They tremble, and well they may.

'Thrice is he armed who hath his quarrel just.'

"It is a beautiful night. The soft breath of evening plays upon my cheek,

> 'Yet on the heart,
> The sense of pleasure presses with a weight,
> That half hath started tears—'tis strange that even
> Our happiness should be so linked with pain!'

"There, I have quoted poetry enough, unless I give you some of my own. But I will not—'I'll be merciful!'"

Capt. Howe called and looked at my arrangements. "I should object to this," said he, "on the ground of expediency." My objections, I assured him, were principally on constitutional grounds.

TUESDAY, Aug. 6, 1839.

A hot morning, and until we had a thunder shower, I could scarcely hold my head up. Letters from two of my fair correspondents. Had a visit from some of my old friends—got out of my cell, and went up to the debtors' rooms. Killed time playing poker, but there was no escaping the heat of the morning. I was in a precious *stew;* and as a *dernier resort,* went to rhyming.

> E'en down in h—ll
> They have a spell
> Sometimes, that isn't hotter
> Than melted lead;
> And once, 'tis said,
> 'Twas cool as boiling water.
>
> But here above,
> O Lord of love,
> Have pity on this nation;
> We're one and all,
> Both great and small,
> Parboiled in perspiration.
>
> O cursed bars!
> Were I at Carr's,
> I'd cooling comfort draw;
> I'd lie in luck
> All day, and suck
> Mint juleps through a straw!

JUG, AUGUST 7, 1839.

TO MY FRIEND ROSALIE, GREETING:—Many thanks for your last kind, beautiful, and most welcome letter.

I thank you too, for your attempted visit. I should have been truly happy to have seen you—to have eaten your fruit, and inhaled the perfume of your flowers. I hope I may see you yet. My lodgings are not very splendid, but they are the best the county can afford me. By some blunder of the contractor, all the joiner work was done by blacksmiths. Fruits and flowers are too great luxuries to be allowed a prisoner. If they knew how much more I value kind and lovely faces, and sweet voices, you would never be admitted. I hope my keepers will be wholly insensible to your attractions; and as all luxuries are excluded, pray don't look any prettier than you can help. Bright as your eyes are, you cannot annihilate my jailer. It is impossible to destroy the smallest particle of matter!

"I probably read less poetry than almost any person who reads it at all. Either because I have little taste for it, or because so little of it comes up to my idea of what poetry should be; and when I try to write it myself, I directly throw down my pen in disgust at the miserable abortions I produce. I was not born a poet, and for months do not write a couplet. I am very doubtful as to the merit of what I do write. At the age of seventeen I wrote a "Poem on Ambition." It was of some one hundred and fifty verses, and thrown off in two hours, by the aid and assistance of a little prepared opium, to help inspiration. I have not taken any since, except for the tooth ache; but shall, if I ever need it, and coffee will not answer my purpose. It was a curious production, beginning with Alexander and ending with Napoleon Buonaparte. I will not be so merciful as you. I feel malignant, and will transcribe all I can remember of it.

* * * * * *

"I used to feel poetry, talk poetry, and live in a world full of glorious poetry; but now I am a jaded, hackneyed, persecuted scribbler of newspaper paragraphs, about the rise of cotton and the fall of stocks—puffs on porter houses, and police reports of loafers in limbo.

"I would that my cheek were quite near yours when the warm breath of evening plays over it so softly. Sometimes it comes over mine, but not with the free, rapturous gush of the zephyrs that wander at large. The very air is imprisoned. I found the 'Captive Knight' this morning and sung it. I heard no clarion, and so played the *fiddle*.

"I have not many correspondents. Since scribbling became my profession, I have not resorted to it for recreation; and he who has to write for thousands every day, finds little opportunity to write for one, unless he get into jail, or some such matter. If I said your letters were faultless, it would be flattery. If I did not say they were beautiful, and for your age, surprisingly well written, I should do you less than simple justice." * * * *

TO MRS. ———.

"Dear Madam:—I was sorry to hear, the other day, of your illness. I hope, ere this, you are recovered, but have no means of ascertaining. Your welfare and happiness will always be dear to me. I have much to thank you for, and many happy hours I owe to you. I was a stranger, and by your fireside I found friendship and affection. Oh! what were this world—brutal, selfish, merciless—without them? You were not the friend of a summer day, merely; but with true constancy, your kindness followed me in all my reverses. Some would call them so, but you know I have always looked upon them as triumphs, and such I firmly hope they will yet prove.

"I think the more highly of the kind attentions you have shown me, from the fact that you have hazarded encountering the shafts of the envious or malignant. The evil minded and the base are ever ready to put the worst constructions upon the best motives and noblest actions, and I have feared that you would be made the subject of some stupid slander; for no character is pure enough to escape it. The reckless defamer loves a high and shining mark to shoot his shafts of venom at; but with those who know you truly, you have nothing to fear." * *

SATURDAY, August 10, 1839.

Indolence and dissipation are stealing away my hours, to the sad neglect of my studies, for which I feel little inclination. I get up, and if locked in, I read, write, and sleep. If my cell chance to be open, I walk about, talk with the prisoners, and play violin duets with Appleby, who plays very well by ear.

At night I sing any thing I can remember—love songs and negro extravaganzas. Then I listen to a trial going on among the prisoners. Every time a new one is brought in, they try him. Each in their separate cells; one acts as judge, another as district attorney, and witnesses are examined, pleas made, and sentences pronounced. This is a standing evening amusement.

The demonstrations of public feeling have been so strong of late, that I am treated with more lenity; but it is still harsh and tyrannical.

My whole imprisonment and the treatment I have received has shocked the feelings of every person of sensibility, and astonished people from one end of the country to the other. Brutal, illegal, and unparalleled in severity, both citizens and strangers consider it an outrage upon humanity, and a disgrace to the city where it can be inflicted with impunity. Every day, almost, people from distant parts of the Union, come to see me; and although my friends, the best and dearest, are excluded, strangers are generally admitted. They express but one opinion, and manifest but one feeling. Among the rest was an intelligent Englishman. He could not restrain his indignation. He said he had been a magistrate in the old country, and was extensively acquainted with judicial proceedings here, and declared that he never knew or heard of an imprisonment in such a case, where the tyranny was so odious; and that in England, any officer who would *dare* to inflict it would not fail of losing his situation. The old man spoke with all the warmth of true, liberal feeling.

Monday, August 12, 1839.

Locked up. Last night I dreamed of blowing up the sheriff in a half hour's speech. It was in language such as I could not command when awake, unless under very strong excitement.

I write but little for the Buffalonian, for, however favorable the monotony of a prison life may be to the prosecution of a continuous story, when fancy supplies the materials, or a work of metaphysical research, or theological controversy, it is but ill adapted to the production of that peculiar kind of literature found in the modern daily newspaper.

Every article should be founded, directly or remotely, upon some present or recent event, some matter of general interest, to which it draws public attention, or to which it has been drawn already. Abstract speculations are out of place, as much so as if a man who met you in the street, should commence a lecture upon the philosophy of Confucius, or the worship of Chrishna.

A newspaper should answer the hourly question, "What's the news?"—or the common ones, "How go the times?"—"What is the state of trade?"—"Is there anything going on?" and "What's the prospect?" These are not questions to be answered from the cell of a prison.

He who expects to find in the columns of a newspaper, depth of research, force of reasoning, splendor of diction, brilliancy of imagination, and all the elegance of elaborate compositions, must generally be disappointed. A daily newspaper is eminently conversational. It is the most familiar species of writing, and differs as much from even a monthly periodical, as the every day calls of a friend do from the occasional, ceremonious, and stately visits of an ordinary acquaintance.

Let it be remembered too, that the daily newspaper is yet in its infancy. It has commenced a new career in a new country. How different are the newspapers of the present day, from those of fifty years since! How much will they yet be improved! Their importance has not been appreciated, but it will be; and men are beginning to learn that the daily press is, and is to be, the great lever of modern civilization and republican liberty.

I did not choose the profession of a newspaper editor, as preferable to every other, without having reflected upon its advantages, its duties, and its responsibilities; nor, having chosen it, shall I give up, but with my existence, the straight forward path I have marked out. Let others prostitute their vile and venal pens to a *clique*, or a party, mine shall be honest and free; and if, in future, corruption and usurpation shall make liberty and law but sounding names, no man shall be able to point to me, and say that I have aided in the unholy work of making slaves of those who were born to the rights of freemen.

JAIL, Tuesday, August 13, 1839.

John Low, one of the gang who tore down my office last spring, has made an affidavit of the facts of the case, implicating some twelve or fifteen of "our first men" of the "infamous clique," in that transaction. It is as I supposed. They planned and paid, the others did the work. A year ago I would not have believed such a thing possible.

I can remember, as if it were yesterday, when I thought men, with a few rare and distant exceptions, were honest, just and benevolent. I remember the shock I felt, when I first heard that one of my neighbors had been convicted of some crime, when

I had to bring the exception nearer home than I had ever supposed could happen.

I lived long in this delusion; and it was not until I had some personal observation of hypocrisy and crime—and I have had more within the last year than during my whole former existence—that I gave credit to stories of human depravity. I have been reluctantly compelled to believe them; and now, instead of thinking all men honest and upright, I have learned to suspect the fairest seeming show.

I have seen meanness allied to wealth, crime covered by a cloak of sanctity, corruption sitting boldly on the bench of justice, and wrong and treachery in every station and under every disguise; but mostly have I seen them in the long, black mantle of hypocrisy.

When will men learn that their truest policy is justice, and their utmost wisdom to do right? When will they be convinced that "corruption wins not more than honesty?"

FRIDAY, Aug. 16, 1839.

To-morrow my time will be just half expired. Two months more of this—then freedom!

I do believe the women have about all the benevolence that is left to this selfish generation. To-day I had an hour's visit from two ladies, both young and pretty, and both strangers. I have met one in the street, I remember, for her form and features are not those a man would forget, but the other I never saw. The one I had seen before, I found particularly interesting. Her eyes sparkled as I talked with her, and when she rose to leave, I could not deny myself, nor did she refuse me, the luxury of a kiss; though all luxuries are so strictly forbidden. I looked round to the other, and then to the one I had just saluted. She smiled—said Yes, as if I had asked a question. Indeed it would not have been polite, not to.

I should have been born in a country where kissing is the fashionable salutation; but I don't like to be bussed by a great, bearded man. Sometimes a foreigner insists upon it, and then I have to submit with as good a grace as possible.

The court is in session. The brick pavement is echoing to the tread of restless feet, and blanched faces are gloomily fixed in sad reflections upon thoughtless follies, rash crimes, or suffered injuries. Hour after hour, that hurried tread is continued, and every time the ringing of the court house bell falls on the ear, it seems to falter for a moment, and then quicken.

Who can tell what thoughts are rushing through the prisoner's brain, while his fate yet hangs suspended on the chances of a trial? Wife, child, father, mother, sister, all may crowd around him. Think of the agony of him whom perchance one hasty, ill-considered act has made a felon! Think too of the bitterness of his reflections, who, guiltless of crime, is sent to a penitentiary. Such there probably are, and with such, the sense of wrong and injustice may be worse than the remorse of guilt. I doubt not it is. The most contented are those who are most guilty.

The weather is delightful, away from the sweltering heat of the prison. In the yard I enjoy a half hour, morning and night, and then return to my cell, my books, and my pen. My muse pays me an occasional visit. This is her last inspiration.

How sweet the breath of summer's morn!
How beautiful yon azure sky!
While silvery clouds, by zephyrs borne,
Sweep in their glorious brightness by.

High walls enclose me—morn and eve,
My cage unbarred, a little space,
I can survey the vault of Heaven;
But none of earth's loved scenes can trace.

The feather'd tenants of the air
    Fly o'er me on their buoyant wings,
Each joyous note, how free from care!
    Wild freedom every warbler sings.

How beautiful the evening hour,
    When Sol puts on his golden vest,
And throwing off his robe of power,
    Sinks to his gorgeous couch of rest.

JAIL, Aug. 17, 1839.

Every day the term of my imprisonment grows shorter, and every day my spirits rise to a higher pitch of vivacity. All before me looks bright with the flattering hues of hope. Spirits of love and bliss hover around me, and in the silence of midnight still my guardian angel ever whispers hope. In the morning I see the walls and fences glittering in the beams of the rising sun, and think of all the splendors of nature, enlightened by his beams; at evening for a few moments his rays light my cell with golden radiance. He sinks below the horizon, and the west is hung with nature's gorgeous drapery. I catch a narrow glimpse of its glory and watch its fading hues. A thousand busy thoughts come clustering about me—dear and happy thoughts of scenes of former joys. It grows dark; and solaced by the lore of sages, and the brilliant imaginings of poets, I wait for the gentle approaches of the drowsy god. I sink to rest, and another day has gone to join the past, nor wholly in vain, for each day leaves behind it some new knowledge, some addition to my store of thought, and some new experience in the vicissitudes of human existence.

Oh! for a pitcher of ice cream, as large as a meeting house! I think I could drink a mint julep, every five minutes. Perhaps one or two didn't come in through the windows this morning. I will not tell who made them. As I drained off the last cold drop, I raised the fragrant glass high in air, and exclaimed,

> Thou prince of caterers! immortal Carr!
> How rich and cooling thy mint juleps are!
> Extatic, thus, the liquid clear to draw,
> Sucked scientifically through a straw!

And Plato dreams that we have lived before, and that now and then we have faint, flitting recollections of a past existence. I have had strange feelings, that startled me sometimes, when I have felt that some event was the fulfilment of a dim remembered prophecy, or the re-acting of some drama almost forgotten, or rather never till then remembered; and when I have felt such, long ago, when my brain was clearer than now, before worldly passions and comminglings, had riled the depths of soul, I wondered at these flitting visions, and thought that Plato might, indeed, reason well. If a future, why not a past? If no end, why a beginning? If immortal, why not eternal?

And in such thoughts as these I spend my days of peaceful meditation. It is sweet sometimes to retire from the bustle of a busy world, and in solitude and silence, commune with one's self, call up the buried past, and form plans for the future. Here, in this snug harbor, sheltered from every storm, my wearied bark reposes from the tossings and tumults of life's tempestuous ocean. All is calm and serene. The sail lays idly by the mast, the loosened cordage hangs in lazy festoons; but soon again upon the open sea of life, she will be proudly ploughing its swelling waves, as, full freighted and buoyant, she

"Now mounts, now totters on the tempest's wing."

SATURDAY, Aug. 18, 1839.

The high fence which has been built around the jail yard, to keep out visiters, does not prevent my hearing the delightful serenades with which my musical friends regale me, almost every pleasant evening. Last night the harmonies of sweet music came

"Still so gently o'er me stealing,"

waking me from slumber like a dream of heaven. "Tara's Harp" swelled in beauty on the calm air of night, and the notes of "Araby's Daughter" died away in cadences of sweet and mournful melody.

It is given out, that upon the least show of a riot in the vicinity of the jail, the U. S. troops will be called out, and the mob dispersed at the point of the bayonet. I wonder if the mayor will not forthwith request a detachment from the barracks to act as a body guard?

The Apprentices' Society have had a benefit, which I am sorry to hear did not amount to much.

Last year the boys came to me, and talked the matter over. I told them they should have a good benefit, and they had one. Capt. Power gave them his boat, and we pushed the matter as it deserved.

The young mechanics of this city must be encouraged. The learned professions do not monopolize mind, and there is no reason why they should the means for its improvement.

The influence of public opinion has mitigated to a considerable extent the rigor of my confinement. Visiters are admitted more freely, and I have managed to smuggle in a small tin boiler, and some ground coffee. Cologne makes a beautiful fuel; and in five minutes I can cook a dish of the fragrant berry better than the best cook in Buffalo.

JAIL, August 20, 1839.

Humanity shudders at the details of distant scenes of cruelty, yet we are too often ignorant of that which is carried on around us. It is an odious feature of the laws in the Spanish West Indies, that makes it dangerous for a man to be a witness of the commission of any crime, as both witness and culprit are confined in the same prison.

A sailor is confined, and has been for a month past, in the jail in this city, and is to be kept, it is said, for some four or five months to come, as a witness to a robbery. He is not in any manner implicated in the transaction, but was sent by the late Mr. Justice Barton, that when the criminals were tried he could be found.

His case is one of great hardship. He is without friends, destitute of clothing, and is losing six months wages; the winter is coming, and though a respectable, good looking young man, his condition is a disgrace to humanity, and beyond the philosophy of most men to endure.

Innocent of any crime, he is thrust into the worst part of the most miserable jail in the state. He lies upon a dirty bunk, with no bed clothes but two filthy blankets, full of vermin, with which he is eaten alive; and all his food is soup made from the offal of the butchers' stalls, and mush, such as farmers make for their swine. His only drink is dirty water, from a shallow, open, rily well, full of filth and insects, from which .forty or fifty prisoners, some of them dirty and lousy beyond description, are every day dipping. And in this situation he lies week after week, that the District Attorney may have a witness, when some poor wretch is to be sent to State Prison.

I have been waked up at midnight by this poor fellow, in an agony of despair, cursing his fate, in terms which nothing but a momentary frenzy could induce, and crying for very madness at the barbarity which thus makes him suffer. The crawling, disgusting vermin, which were eating him up, had waked him from his unquiet sleep. It was terrible to lay in darkness, and a silence only relieved by groans and the clank of fetters, and hear a fellow creature in such misery.

It is true that my diet, my water, my cell, are like his. Kind fortune has given me friends who have provided me with lodgings somewhat more comfortable, and I have managed to keep my bedding free from vermin. I have also firmness of mind, which enables me to bear my confinement with fortitude, and a cheerfulness of disposition which makes me happy under every circumstance, where my sympathies are not every hour awakened for others sharing the same fate, with less ability to sustain it.

That any human being, innocent of crime, should be in such a situation is a disgrace to this city, a disgrace to the county, and its officers. How has the grand jury performed its duties? and how does the the sheriff discharge his? Let the situation of this poor, friendless sailor answer. I scorn to complain for myself, but I cannot see others so wretched.

Imprisonment for crimes the most odious and revolting were bad enough; but it is a far more bar-

barous outrage to put a man, innocent of any crime, in such a place as this, where he lies in

> "Uncomforted
> And friendless solitude, groanings and tears,
> And savage faces at the clanking hour;
> Circled with evil, till his very soul
> Unmoulds its essence, hopelessly deformed
> By sights of evermore deformity."

If such be not the invariable result, it is only because some have **within** them the strong repellant power of virtue. In such

> "The self approving mind is its own light,
> And life's best warmth still radiates from the heart,
> Where love sits brooding, and an honest purpose."

JAIL, Wednesday, Aug. 21, 1839.

"Why don't you write more?" they ask me. I wish every one who propounds this query, could be shut up a few weeks in a dark hole, eight feet long by five feet wide, and high in proportion, and fed on shin soup and mush. Lord bless their simple souls! Write? let them try it.

I do write; but not copy for newspapers. I write poetry. Here are eight lines I wrote yesterday, the first time trying, and christened the sentimental and enormous production,

THE PILLOW OF LOVE.

> Love's pillow is fair woman's breast,
> His zephyrs are her gentle sighs,
> Her breath the perfume he loves best,
> And his loved light her radiant eyes.
>
> Does Love want roses? Heavenlier hues
> Are glowing on her cheeks and lips;
> She smiles—rubies and pearls he views,
> And kisses for his nectar sips.

Then I keep a Journal. I do better than write, I study. In no two months of my life, did I ever learn so much. It is better than all treasures. Gold cannot buy it. One hundred and fifty dollars is cheap tuition in such a boarding school. As our little Dutchman says, I like it *very mush*.

Time does not hang one moment heavily upon me. I have a variety of resources. I write—when I can't write, I read. If poetry won't do, I try prose—if history wearies, I resort to fiction; if none will do, I can fiddle, sing or dance; and when in the lonely night I wake, and the hot, stifling air is pressing around me, and my head is too feverish for rest, I make a light, and write, as now, or read myself to sleep again; and then again I lay and think—think—think.

So pass my days and nights. 'Tis a long voyage, but I have pleasant companions. There is Gibbon, the prince of historians, who in his grand historic style, discourses by the hour, of the decline and fall of the Roman Empire; a glorious theme of a great mind. Next comes the great Doctor Johnson; and he tells me of poets and distinguished men, and repeats over stores of critical learning and philosophy. In walks Dean Swift, sullen and satirical. Coleridge, metaphysically poetical, pours his wild warblings into my listening spirit; Shelley opens his noble heart, so full of love and freedom; wild, warbling, wicked Tom Moore sings me gay songs of love and rapture, or tells me tales of Eastern Lands, all full of flashing gems and glowing flowers. The transcendant Shakspeare too sometimes spends an hour with me, and the thoughtful, gay courtier, and misanthropic poet, Young.

Then there are Sir Edward Lytton Bulwer, and the eloquent young D'Israelli, the prolific James, and the mirth-provoking Dickens. Have I not, for company, a glorious set of fellows? A man who could not be happy in such society, should never go to jail, I can tell him that.

Nor are these all. Every day, along comes my pursy, poetical friend "Horatio;" but just now he is splitting his big sides crowing over democratic victories; and almost every day comes the dark Doctor, looking blacker than usual from the same cause. Occasionally there comes the ray of "sun" light too, but not bright enough to require smoked glass to look at it.

Then strangers call sometimes. There is a fine looking old Knickerbocker makes me, once a month, a very delightful visit; and if ladies are not allowed to see me, I sometimes get quite cosey with a "Ladies' Companion." Without paying much regard to my person, I am sure of having a "New York Mirror" once a week. Every day a "Herald" arrives with the latest news, and I catch the "Spirit of the Times." Several other distinguished personages, I have sent invitations to, and am every day expecting. Among these are my old friend Cervantes, Le Sage, Fielding, Smollett, and old Burton. I should likewise be much pleased with a visit from the wizard Sir Walter, and a certain dissolute but clever Lord.

Lonely? Why, here is the choicest company. Difficult indeed must be the man who wants better than these, and a free opportunity to enjoy their conversation. I show my independence by treating these distinguished and worthy gentlemen quite cavalierly. I don't stand bowing and paying compliments, but if I want to talk about the happy valley with the rough old Doctor, I catch hold of him, and hand him along to where I am sitting or lying, without the least ceremony. And when I have had enough of him, I tell him to just "shut up," and make room for somebody else.

To suppose all this is not very delightful, is the greatest mistake in the world; and I am astonished that any person should presume to pity me.

JAIL, August 22, 1839.

Delightful letters from three of my fair correspondents. There is no reasoning with a woman; that I found out long since. They will be the creatures of impulse and passion—will love, hate and be jealous; and sometimes behave very naughtily; but they are enough better than the men. I never knew a woman who could be a cool, systematic villain. The very word is of the masculine gender. So are rascal, knave, scoundrel. Who ever thought of applying either of these terms to a woman?

The worst fault I have to find with women is their injustice to each other. If one of them yields to an impulse of God's own giving, without going through the formalities of custom, they do not say, "Go and sin no more," or try to win her to virtuous conduct. She is driven from society, and no matter how beautiful, how accomplished or how good—no matter how sincerely she regrets her folly, or how ardently she longs to live in the ways of virtue, she is made an outcast—

"Doomed to know
Polluted nights and days of blasphemy,
Who in loathed orgies, with lewd wassailers
Must gaily laugh, while the remembered home
Gnaws like a viper at her secret heart."

And she is hunted to her lonely and dishonored grave. Do women right in this? Is chastity in one sex no virtue, and its violation in the other the only vice that cannot be forgiven? Is there any remedy? None; while women behave towards each other so cruelly. These reflections have been prompted by a letter I received yesterday, from one of the class of whom Coleridge wrote the above lines, and whose talents, beauty and moral worth, would have done honor to any station. She writes confidentially to me, for she knows my sentiments.

"They think it a very easy matter for a girl who is placed in my situation to reform if they wish to; but let the lady who thinks so, but be placed in similar circumstances. Let her become an outcast from society and her character generally known. Let the door of her own dear home be barred against her—let her descend from one stage to another, until she is sunk to the lowest abyss of ignominy; then let her think of reforming. Let it be the dearest object, the fondest wish of her soul. Let her feel willing to labor day and night, to exchange situations with the poorest servant girl in the world, to put up with all the inconveniences and hardships attendant on a life of poverty and obscurity, if she could only be respectable; and then let her learn that it is an impossibility—that if woman chances to swerve from the strictest rules of virtue,—

> 'Ruin ensues, reproach and endless shame;
> And one false step forever blasts her fame.
> In vain with tears the loss she may deplore,
> In vain look back to what she was before,
> Like stars from Heaven fallen to rise no more!'"

And such is the truth. I know an instance where a beautiful and gifted girl was sold to the embraces of a rich libertine. She won the love of a talented young man, who ranked high in his profession. He married her, and she was true to her plighted faith, and conducted herself to the admiration of all who knew her. Was she received into society, and encouraged in such a laudable reformation? No. One would suppose *Christians* would try to act in accordance with the example of Christ, and the precepts of his gospel. Verily all this is not right.

"Let him that is without sin among you, cast the first stone;" said the blessed Redeemer to the Scribes and Pharisees, who brought to him the woman taken in adultery; thus teaching, to them, and to all future generations, a lesson of charity, the holiest and noblest ever taught to erring humanity.

Men, and men who call themselves christians, too often forget this heavenly lesson, and while they pray for pardon from Heaven, as they forgive those that have trespassed against them, yet cherish malice and revenge in their hearts. Will such prayers be heard? Forgetting the weakness and frailty of human nature — forgetting their own manifold offences, they who are deepest in the mire of pollution, are often the first to condemn others.

It is a painful—most pitiful characteristic of thousands; a savage, brutal propensity, that, when a fellow creature has by the force of circumstances, or his own depravity, been hurried into crime, and becomes involved in its consequences, they will turn upon him with the ferocity of so many fiends, and crush him down to ruin—men too, who have, perhaps, been guilty of the same or more heinous crimes, men who ought to be the last to condemn a fellow being.

If I ever condemn a man for his misdeeds, it is while he is in the full career of successful villany; not when he is struck down, and the world turns against him. Then heavenly pity intervenes; and charity, the sublimest christian virtue, the one without which all other gifts and graces are of no avail, comforts the wounded spirit, and visits the guilty and forsaken one with the balm of consolation. I have not an enemy on earth, that in the hour of trouble and adversity I would not succor and console.

If this be a duty, where there is no doubt in regard to the guilt, how much more should both humanity and justice teach forbearance towards those whose guilt is yet **unproved**, and how careful should we be not to **obstruct** or thwart the course of impartial justice. *Fiat justitia ruat cœlum,* should be an universal motto. It cannot be too hackneyed.

I think I will go to writing sermons, and lecturing on moral reform. But to-night enough. The world will go on in its old track. It is useless to check the torrent of popular prejudices, which sweeps over every thing, and often carries with it ruin and desolation.

FRIDAY, Aug. 23, 1839.

Mr. R. from Syracuse, called to see me. We had a profitable season together. When I came to Buffalo, where he then resided, he was one of the first men I got acquainted with, and there are few I more highly esteem. When we shook hands at parting, he left in my hand a V, and I could find no words to thank him.

The weather or some other cause has taken away my appetite. I eat nothing and have grown quite attenuated. My cheeks have lost their color, and my face looks absolutely ghastly. My strength fails me too, and all desire for exercise. The soup and mush is sent back untasted, for in truth it is not fit to be eaten. The worst punishment I wish for those who provide it, is for them to live upon it a few months in one of these cells; and my conscience gives a twinge of reproach at the cruelty of that.

I have read Shelley's Revolt of Islam. Shelley was a most amiable and enthusiastic philanthropist. His whole soul was full of the spirit of liberty.

Last night I had a beautiful serenade. I waked from a feverish sleep, lighted my candle, and listened. Then I took down my violin and echoed the air. "Good night, Nichols;" said my unknown minstrels. "Good night," I cried, and sunk again to rest. I looked at my watch; it was half past two.

I have plenty of newspapers. There is a great crop of wheat in Michigan. When a year ago I told people flour would be down to five dollars a barrel, they laughed at me. Wait till next winter. The country, according to the political papers, is on the crater of a volcano. It has been in that same perilous situation ever since the Revolution. There is a pane of glass in Boston, so large that it takes four men to look through it. Three tried and couldn't do it. A newspaper writer calls the lower world the Texas of eternity. This is evidently a gross libel either on Hell or Texas. This is all the news by the last mails.

TUESDAY, Aug. 27, 1839.

Summer is fading into autumn. Already the nights grow cold, and the other morning the plants showed signs of frost. Soon the glowing season of vegetative life will be over. The fruits will ripen, and be garnered into plenteous stores; the withering leaf will be hurried on the chilly breeze, away from the parent stem. Each once glowed in beauty, a world of animated life, covered with tiny beings—a miscroscopic nation, that rose and fell in a single summer.

How wonderful thou art, O Nature! How broad thy page, how countless thy lessons! Are they all spread out for us? Is it for us weak, puny creatures, that myriads of worlds whirl ceaselessly through the regions of boundless space? Is it for us that the whole creation teems with existence, and with mind? For us each plant is covered with its generations of animalculæ, and earth, air, and ocean teem with forms of beautiful and joyous being? How small and insignificant a portion of creation are we, and yet how dignified, how noble above all others that we know, and how depraved below. Great in our knowledge and our depravities, great in our virtues and our crimes, we stand alone among the earthly creatures of the Almighty.

Wednesday, Aug. 28, 1839.

I am absolutely too indolent to copy my letters. There is a heap of them, from my dear correspondents. Blessings on him who invented letter writing. I must answer the last; and first, a

LETTER TO ROSALIE.

"MY FRIEND ROSALIE:—I think I have missed one of your letters. You may congratulate yourself on one of mine having miscarried; for it contained two mortal sheets of rhymes and nonsense.

"I have still seven weeks to remain in jail; by my soul, 'a very pretty prospect ahead;' and yet to see me, you would think me one of the most thoughtless, contented and happy beings in the universe, and so I sometimes think I am. Yesterday, I smuggled in a hot beef steak and cup of coffee. The steak made me ill, and the coffee kept me awake all night; so altered is the tone of my system, by confinement and semi-starvation. I shall have to be very careful when I get out.

"One of my dear little girls called yesterday and spent an hour with me, amusing me with her conversation, and innocent endearments. She is eleven years old, and a bright and lovely creature. This afternoon I had a visit from two beautiful girls, a few years older—still you do not come. Since then, I have given myself up to a fit of fiddling; and for the last hour have been improvising songs, to the infinite amusement of my fellow prisoners.

"It is half past six, P. M., and we are all locked in our cells; my candle is lighted, and the prisoners are talking or singing songs, not always of the most refined character. The following is all I can remember of one of their favorites.

'In Dubling city I was bred and born—
On Stephen's Green I die forlorn;
'Twas there I learned the saddler's trade;
But was always counted a roving blade.
  Chorus. 'Twas there, &c.

At seventeen I took a wife;
I loved her dearly as I loved my life,
And to maintain her both neat and gay,
I took to robbin on the highway.
  Chorus. And to maintain, &c.'

"This is set to a beautiful and plaintive melody, and the chorus is sung with great unction. Songs of robbers, pirates, and prisons are the favorites.

"For my part, I prefer negro songs, and generally sing a dozen, whenever I am in humor. Among these elegant productions of musical and poetic genius are Clar de Kitchen, Settin on a Rail, Zip Coon, Sich a gittin up Stairs, Jim Brown, Gumbo Chaff, Jim

Crow, and several others that I learned "long time ago," with that exquisite parody,

>'De Jaw Bone hung in de kitchen hall,
>De Sea Bass scale shine on de ole wall,
>Ole Possum's brack friends lub fun and were gay,
>An dey kick up de debble on a holiday.'

"The airs are admirably adapted to improvisation, and my violin is turned into a banjo with the utmost facility.

"Then I lay down, and with the aid of ventriloquism, get Patrick into a violent quarrel, with a blackguardly countryman of his, on the outside, who, he fancies, has come under the window to abuse him; and very wrathy he gets, and very much he wants to get out and fight the rascal; and all this goes on amid roars of laughter, and I condole with Patrick, and then abuse him for a beggarly thief of a Paddy, with impunity, by throwing my voice out of the window. The other night I made him think one of the prisoners was strangling himself in his cell, and he called lustily for the jailer. There is an old blacksmith a few doors from me. He has been put in for making "bogus," when the Lord knows, and the District Attorney would if he had common sense, that he is innocent of the necessary knowledge. When he was first brought here, he looked round with a long face, and with an inimitable drawl, said, 'Well! this don't look much like home.' He sits day after day, reading Bunyan's Holy War, and the Bible; and sometimes his little children come to see him. Towards night, he asks the time of some one who wears a watch, and says—'Well, another day is most gone—I hope Mr. Nichols will *perform* to-night!' So I perform as aforesaid, and sometimes I make a speech, on human rights and liberty, or deliver a lecture to the ball and chain gang on metaphysics, practical ethics, and psychology, with some arguments in favor of the metempsichosis, and the probability of universal infinity, to their wonderful edification.

"Such are some of my philosophical amusements. I am reading Shelley, pencil in hand, and collecting a vast store of literary prettinesses and sublimities, and am also very busy, cultivating a pair of whiskers, which I hope to get so far forward as not to be affected by the early frosts.

"When shall I begin author, and write my first novel? The time has not come yet. When it does, you will see, what you will see.

"I would tear this up, only that it will take me just as long to write another, which may be even less endurable; and I shall also have to wait longer for your answer."

JAIL, August 30, 1839.

LETTER TO JULIA.

"I have had no opportunity to send to you before for several days, but unexpected ones, of which, owing to my negligence, I could not avail myself. Your letters are always acceptable. I like to hear from all my friends, but to hear you are well, gives me emotions of peculiar pleasure. Why not be candid with me? You may confide in me; and whatever I may appear to others, I am not unworthy of your confidence, and the regard you have avowed for me. I would read every page of your heart. Do tell me all you feel, and let us be friends indeed.

"I am glad it is in my power to give you any pleasure; and yet I sometimes think it might have been better, had you never known me. You might have been happier; and yet, have we not enjoyed some delicious hours? If your heart speaks like mine, it will answer, yes. I know not why, but the more I become acquainted with you, the more I esteem you. You are superior to the generality of your sex, in mind and feeling. You are superior to the stupid envy and malignity of common natures. Free from their groveling tastes, independent of the world's opinion, you are at liberty to enjoy the highest pleasures of existence, and may live in a perpetual atmosphere of love and happiness.

"It is not necessary to rudely break the chains of custom, so that the world may hear the jar and see the ruin. They may be more cautiously unlinked; or worn so easily, that while we seem bound, we may be as free as the loftiest nature could desire. It will not do to set the god, Fashion, at defiance. He is a potent deity, and we must appear to pay him our devotions, while in our hearts, we worship Liberty, a brighter divinity. It is the only way. The dictates of the heart are hidden, and may be secretly followed. The mandates of Fashion and Custom are open, and must be obeyed.

"For my own sake I am sorry to hear that you leave Buffalo this fall; but I doubt not you will be happier, where you are going. I shall miss you much, but I never had a dear friend who did not leave me. You will not forget me; and when fate joins your destiny to that of the favored one, whom you will love most devotedly, for you would not marry without, there will be still one little corner of your heart left for me. I should not love you less than now, for I am the most constant of poetical and platonic lovers. There is in my affections no 'shadow of turning.' Wherever you go, may you be happy."

* * * * * *

MORE ALBUM VERSES.

TO J * * *

Fair girl, I've looked with rapture on thine eyes of sparkling light,
I've gazed upon thy cheeks' rich glow, thy neck of dazzling white,
And Oh! I've thought, while near thee, I have seen thy bosom swell,
How fondly I could love thee, girl, how dearly and how well.

But I've suppressed the feeling that was rising in my breast,
What my eyes were still revealing, my lips have ne'er expressed.
My girl, I must not love thee, yet I cannot tell thee why;
Oh! wilt thou read that line as it is written, with a sigh?

And yet, I would not part with thee, I'd claim thee for a friend,
Ask thee, the sunlight of thy smiles with my dark fate to blend,
Around my aching brow a wreath of Hope's bright flowers to bind,
For thou art young and beautiful, I know that thou art kind.

Fair girl, will this content thee? wilt thou grant the fond request,
And give unto my cup of life its most enduring zest?
Love, Oh! I deeply feel it, is a passion wild and vain,
And for each moment's pleasure brings us hours of grief and pain.

I never will deceive thee—Oh! I could not cause a tear
To dim the brightness of thine eye, whose every glance is dear;
Be but my kind and loving friend, my sister, and I'll prove
So fond and true, that thou'lt confess, 'tis better far than love.

SATURDAY EVENING, Aug. 31, 1839.

How often, when free, shall I turn over these pages, and think of all the incidents of my imprisonment! Perhaps I will read them aloud to some dear friend. I have got the best ghost story I ever heard. The circumstance happened but a few days ago, and I had it this afternoon from the lips of the young lady to whom the apparition appeared. To be sure, I have heard an hundred similar ones, and in a few instances have known the party; but in the relator of this I have the greatest confidence.

She was standing near her door, just at twilight, when she saw, a short distance from her, a gentleman with whom she was intimately acquainted. A young lady near her saw him also. She walked toward him, wished him "good evening," and asked him to come in. He declined, but asked her to walk; and though she urged him again, still he refused to come into the house. They walked slowly down toward the lake shore, crossing one of the canal bridges, conversing upon different subjects. His manner appeared abstracted, but not so odd as to cause her any surprise.

Having arrived at the beach, they sat down on a log, which the last gale had thrown upon the sand, and enjoyed the beauty of the evening. The moon was just rising. There was little conversation, and none that she remembered. He raised one of his hands in a singular manner, and laid it on her head. It felt heavy, like a lump of lead, or rather as a dead man's might. That was the last she remembered.

When she came to herself she was lying by the side of the log, on the sand just at the water's edge. The moon was riding high in the heavens, and the night breeze came chilly across the water.

She hastened home, and while going heard the clock of the Old First strike three. The next day, upon inquiry, she found that the gentleman whom she had supposed the companion of her walk had left town several days before, nor has he yet returned. She was astonished, but, she assures me, not the least frightened. It seems strange—she cannot account for it, nor can I.

Optical illusions don't talk often, nor are they ever seen by two persons at the same time. I do not think she would deceive me.

IN JAIL, SEPT. 1, 1839.

Rosalie writes—"I quite agree with you, in your opinion of Pelham. It is written by a master hand. Which of Bulwer's heroines do you like best? There is the beautiful and intellectual Ellen Glanville; the high souled, yet gentle Isora Alvares; the devoted Isabel Mordaunt; the sweet wild flower, Lucy Brandon; the noble Lady Flora; the spirited Madeline Lester; just what her name expresses, the proud bride of Rienzi, and his lovely sister, the beautiful Irene; the haughty and wayward Florence Lascelles; the guileless and confiding Evelyn Cameron; the almost angel, Alice—and there is another—sweet Gertrude Vane. It is strange that I should have forgotten her, who have loved her character so well. It is wonderful that for a moment her beautiful memory should have fled from me. And now tell me which one in that galaxy of beauty and goodness you admire most. * * * *

"I have been reading Nicholas Nickleby. Am I very far out of the way, when I say Dickens is one of the greatest writers of the age? I almost think he is; any way, he will make me laugh heartier, and cry oftener than any body else. Do you not think his style of pathos is perfect? There is no mock sentiment, no straining after effect. It is all simple, touching, and natural; and there is now and then a dash of the beautiful, which makes his works perfectly delightful.

* * * * * *

"And now, my friend, let me entreat you to be of good cheer—to be light hearted and gay, even though you are in a lonely cell. You can be happy there. Remember that a thousand hearts beat with indignation at your oppressions, and with admiration for the fearless independence which induced you to uphold the innocent and denounce the guilty." * * * *

LETTER TO ROSALIE.

"I would that I had fitting words, my amiable friend, to thank you for the pleasure your last letter gave me; the happiness occasioned by the perusal of which, was so mingled with admiration for all that is excellent in your heart and understanding, that I scarcely know whether I was more struck by its beauty, or grateful for the feelings which induced you to write it. You know what I mean; I believe I do not express myself very felicitously.

"You have put me a very puzzling question, and I fear I shall let myself down in your estimation by my answer. I have read all of Bulwer's novels but two. Some of them many years since, others recently; but my memory of most of his heroines, I am sorry to say, is dim and ill defined. Strange as it may seem, I remember his heroes much better, and those not too well. I beg the ladies' pardons, but I have not the honor of their acquaintance. I may have admired them all while reading of them, but they made no abiding impression. And yet, in real life I never forget a beautiful face or form that I have ever seen, though but a moment, in the street. Of novels *written by men*, I remember the heroes better than the heroines. For instance, I know Pelham, much better than Ellen, whose beauty and excellence I recall with an effort; but lady Roseville I remember better; and while Rienzi stands out in bold relief in my memory, I had even forgotten that he had a bride. So of Devereux and his lady love.

18 *

"You should not despise Florence Lascelles. You are too young to judge her, and would never speak harshly of her had you ever loved. I have nothing to say of Maltravers, but I am slow to condemn men for faults of passion; for those of meanness and cupidity I have no mercy.

"In the case of —— I have been polite; and as she is very pretty and very kind, perhaps a little more. I love her as I do all my friends; and when I give way to my feelings, I fear they may be mistaken. Now do not accuse me of vanity in this. It is simple experience. I would not for a moment excite hopes that must be disappointed. You women, I know not how it is, want to monopolize a man. He must love you and love no other, or straight you get jealous, and there is the devil to pay, and your little hearts break; but thank Heaven they almost always get mended again. Now I never, *if I can help it*, will deceive a lady in such a matter. If she insist upon loving me, I will try to love her as well as I can; but I will never deliberately try to win love, where I cannot return it, nor raise anticipations I can never fulfil. Now were all as sensible as you, there would be no trouble. They would never mistake friendship for love; but I am writing a lecture, on what, though you have read a great deal, you know very little about."

JAIL, Thursday, Sept. 5.

Thus far my Journal. I have had a great many visiters. Many of them ladies. Some very beautiful and very dear ones. I wish women could love without being jealous. I can't contrive how they manage in Turkey and the whole Eastern world.

Cooper brought me a bunch of magnificent Dahlias. They want but perfume to make them perfect. A friend has brought me the latest novels.

One of these is the "Barber of Paris," by Paul de Kock, remarkable for its strong lights and shades, forming vivid, beautiful or grotesque portraitures, and its fine illustrations of the manners of the age of Richelieu.

The "Gentleman of the Old School," by James, is in many respects an excellent novel, full of incident, and involved in its plot, which is quite dramatic.

The author remarks, when a plot is maturing for depriving an innocent man of liberty, to gratify a selfish scoundrel, and in which he found but too willing instruments in the officers of the law,

"The words justice, the course of law, proper punishment, &c. &c. &c., have in all ages been made to cover every sort of iniquity and persecution."

"Juries have been," says the scoundrel to the magistrate —"juries have been — I say, Sir, juries, have been——"

"I know they have, Sir," replied Mr. Waters, coming to his assistance; "*arranged*, you mean; managed a little—prejudiced people excluded, and impartial people put in, by a little *dexterous manœuvering;*—and I have a mortgage on the estate of Mr. ——, who wants a little time to pay the interest," &c. &c.

They got the hero in prison, where he went very willingly; and the author remarks, "forgot to calculate the weary hours of imprisonment—forgot to calculate how terrible would be the close restraint of a dull jail, to one who had never known any thing but freedom."

The under-sheriff, it appears, was a gentleman, forming a remarkable contrast to some officers with whom I have the honor of being acquainted.

" 'We will give you our best room, Captain,' said the governor (of the prison;) 'and I think you can't have a more comfortable one in all England.' But when, having led the way and unlocked the door, he ushered Stafford in, and the young gentleman met the close, foul, unventilated atmosphere of the small, narrow room in which he was to spend many a weary day, he felt still more strongly what a prison is; and the *dark, painful, degrading lesson,* was concluded and confirmed in a minute after, by the harsh turning of the heavy lock, which shut him from his fellow creatures."

The magistrate aforesaid makes other observations, equally shrewd and pertinent.

" 'I think there is a chance of getting hold of any man one likes,' replied Waters; 'thank God, the laws of this country, if properly managed, give one great facilities.' * * * * * *

"As they passed the prison, Mr. Forrest looked up with a feeling of vengeful satisfaction.

"But could he have looked into the bosom of the person who sat solitary within those walls, and compared what he saw there, sad and gloomy as it was, with the state, the feelings, the dark writhings of his own spirit, the voice of conscience would have told him, It is thou that art punished!"

SEPTEMBER 6, 1839.

I do think I wrote as pretty a piece of extravagance and egotism for to-day's Buffalonian, as often gets into a newspaper. Here is a little specimen.

"I am perfectly conscious that there is not one single particle of meanness, dishonesty, or vice in my composition. This is reason enough why those who are wholly made up of these beautiful qualities, should so fear and persecute me. I know myself to be honest, upright, talented, and virtuous, and especially the latter, which is the principal reason, that and my modesty, the modesty that always accompanies genius, why the blessed and lovely women, from the sweet, dove-eyed little girls, to the benevolent, spectacled old ladies, are all my warm friends and most eloquent champions.

"Now, all that is the truth—the holy, simple, beautiful, unadultered truth, and yet there are not three men in the United States who *dare* to write so. I will write the truth now and always, so help me God. The politicians, and the *clique*, the robbers of the living and dead, may lie—and lie. I won't lie for any man, not if they chain me. It is strange men will be mean and contemptible, when they would feel so much better, enjoy life with so much higher zest, and eat and drink and sleep, which is the life of the many and the relaxation of the few, with so much higher pleasure, if they acted honorably.

"I have no secrets. The world, the whole world, and Heaven, and the regions of torment are welcome to know all about me. I dreamed I was in hell once, and I felt very much as I did when I came to jail, cool, calm, and rather comfortable than otherwise. I expected the devils along, just as I might be expecting Brace or Brown here this afternoon, and was going to give them a fine blowing up, as I have to do them once in a while.

"But ere they came—before I had the pleasure of seeing a single tail of them, I woke up, with the glorious sun-beams of a bright, fresh morning in Spring, shining through my eyelids, and all the trees were glittering with spray, and the blythe birds singing in the branches; and I listened to the sighing of the gentle breeze, through a grove of tall pines on the hill side, and the roar of a distant torrent, and gazed upon the rich green fields, and the venerable and bald-headed old mountains, and the pure, bright sky, that was spread out like a great canopy above me; and I looked up to heaven, where God, and the Savior, and holy angels are, and the spirits of all the good; and I thought they all smiled upon me, and the great Jehovah seemed to promise me, by all the beauty and loveliness of the world around me, and by the pure and happy feelings that were rising in my own heart, and bursting from my lips in aspirations of praise, that his high home should be my eternal dwelling place, and I should be forever near the glories of his holy throne."

SATURDAY, Sept. 7, 1839.

It is confidentially believed by many, that I shall be kept in prison for a year to come; and I shall not be greatly surprised if they do. Nothing in the course of judicial proceedings can astonish me now. The arm of justice is paralyzed, and the laws are but the instrument of the wicked and corrupt.

Mr. F. called to-day. He had bought a new and splendid album for his wife, in which I had the honor of scribbling first. I never saw the lady—but wrote as off-hand and rapidly as I write every thing, the following lines:

A stranger, lady, writes the first rude line,
  In this rich token of thy husband's love,
Pays his heart's homage to an unknown shrine,
  To thy best friend, his friendship true to prove.

Here is a dreary prison's lonely cell,
  Cramped and confined by massive walls, all round:
Iron-barred doors and clanking fetters tell
  How safely all, but the free soul, is bound.

That is not fettered! as on eagle's wings
 It soars unawed into the fair blue sky,
Above the golden clouds it fearless springs
 And gazes on the Sun of Liberty!

Nor less it roams o'er all the lovely earth,
 Seeking the Beautiful, the Good, the True;
And in imagination's pictured worth,
 Fondly it hails them all combined in you.

Though dark and dreary is my present fate,
 Cheerless my prison, hard my daily fare,
Some cheering rays shine through the dungeon's grate,
 And bid me combat still the fiend Despair.

Lady, farewell! forgive the mingled strain,
 For Hope still gleams where dark Misfortune lowers;
The bright enchantress soothes each present pain,
 And in the future points to happier hours.

Oh! may that future be, to thee and thine,
 Full to the sparkling brim with love and joy;
Still may earth's blessings with heaven's hopes combine,
 And thine be happiness, without alloy.

TO EDWARD.

* * * "A correspondent of the Liberator, I think, calls ministers 'a contemptible and time-serving set.' I do not think that is polite. I do think they are often ignorant; but in religion,

'Where ignorance is bliss! 'tis folly to be wise,'

I sometimes think. Indeed, I have been tempted to envy the ignorant, or, what is the same thing, the prejudiced and bigoted, their credulity.

"The christianity of our day, my brother, is a sad piece of mummery. We need more reformers. Both priests and professors are making religion contemptible. We have a set of the latter, in Buffalo, whose conduct would go far to convert the world to infidelity.

"In regard to the evidences of christianity, I have read very little on either side; and am content to let death decide the matter whenever it may please the Almighty. I have no fears for the future, nor any very strong hopes; I wish for an immortal existence, and try hard to believe in a future state. Conscious of the rectitude of my motives and conduct, I cannot fear a hereafter.

"You are right in not being hasty in beginning the world. Experience will do you no harm. I have been, and am being educated in a rough school. My qualities of firmness, perseverance, and cool determination are increasing in strength, while my mind is every day adding to its stores, and improving its powers.

"However we may be separated, or whatever differences of opinion may divide us, my brother, let us always love each other; and let our highest aim be the welfare and happiness of our fellow creatures."

JAIL, Sept. 9, 1839.

Went out of the jail, and to the grand jury room. Swore a little, and came back. Evidence wanted against the accessories to a certain burglary, and doubts arising whether enough will be had to endict them.

A little boy is calling "mother," fifty times repeated, from the outside of the jail. The mother is locked up, for refusing to testify. This was contempt of court. If all who hold the Recorder's Court in contempt are sent to jail, few of our citizens will remain at liberty.

Pretty girl sent to jail for exposing her infant, leaving it on a rich man's door step. They want to send her to State Prison. She is fainting and hysterical.

A lady whom I never saw, has sent me a basket of provisions. They were smuggled in beautifully, by a very pretty girl.

WEDNESDAY, Sept. 11, 1839.

As I expected, the conspirators were not endicted. Ferris, and Spink, my foreman, are being tried for a libel on Gen. Potter, about which I feel more anxious, than I did when tried myself.

W.'s time is out, but he wants to get rid of his fine. He and I have been very good neighbors. He had a violent prejudice against me, but got over it in a day or two, as most people do, when they come to know me.

There are some half dozen old fellows in jail, sent by their wives for alleged ill treatment. Two or three of them are ugly enough to be convicted of any thing. When their wives got them out of the way, they showed their good taste.

Got a letter from Solomon Southwick, Esq., of Albany; an excellent writer, and an honest man. He says—

"I am glad to see that you bear your imprisonment manfully. I think your case a hard one, because, in the first place, I am decidedly and inflexibly opposed to all criminal prosecutions for libel. A private action for satisfaction in the shape of damages, is the only suit that ought ever to be allowed in such cases, especially in a free country. If any man has received damage at the hands of an editor, by way of libel, he is justly entitled to remuneration in proportion to the damage sustained; and here ought to be, as it is in the eye of common sense, the beginning and end of the law. It is an affair between two individuals, in which the public have no further concern, than merely to see that retributive justice be done to the party injured. Public criminal suits against editors or other writers, were in the first place unquestionably the offspring of some tyrant on the throne, or some tyrant or sycophant, or both, on the bench. The reason assigned for them by Blackstone, and other elementary law authors, is an absurd one, having no foundation in sound ethics or philosophy of any kind. It is indeed a shallow reason, the invention of some selfish or stupid tyrant.

A man is justified in maintaining his reputation or rights in a court of justice; but even in that case, where his reputation alone is concerned, I do not think he ought to appropriate the money obtained to his own use; for it looks too much like making a speculation out of his character.

"But to fine and imprison a libeller under a criminal proceeding, has every appearance of a malicious and revengeful application or perversion of a bad law; and none but bad men will ever act on malicious and revengeful principles. In your case I do not hesitate to say that the punishment is excessive. Four months imprisonment and a fine of $150, for publishing what an editor believes to be true, though it turn out to be false, is, in my opinion, a blow at the liberty of the press, which no independent friend to the rights of his country and of mankind, can either approve or defend.

"In the second place, your case is a hard one, because, whilst you are thus severely punished for libelling the Recorder, (for I am willing to allow for argument's sake that you were in that case a gross libeller,) the base and infamous ruffians and burglars who broke into your office, at midnight, and destroyed your printing materials, instead of being sent to the State Prison, as they ought to have been, were let off with a punishment so light, that it amounted to no punishment at all! If it be the law of Buffalo, to imprison an editor for a libel, four months as a criminal, and fine him excessively besides, while midnight robbers and ruffians are only fined, and not imprisoned at all, but suffered to go at large, it is, to say the least, un-*common* instead of *common law*—it is law without justice; and the sooner Buffalo gets rid of such law, the better will it be for her prosperity at home, and her reputation abroad. She is too full of good, patriotic and enterprising citizens—too much the seat of civilization, art, science, piety and refinement in morals and manners, to suffer such a stain to rest upon her.

"The *editorial corps* is too much divided, I fear, to come together and take an honorable stand for their own rights, and the rights of their country, as it respects the liberty of the press. But some effort ought to be made to shield the press for ever from all public or criminal prosecutions. For in bad times, and under the paramount influence of bad men, there can be no more powerful engine of oppression— nothing more destructive of legal and constitutional rights than such prosecutions.

"They suit precisely the times, the temper and the principles, of such judges as the marble-headed, and infamous Jeffries, and such base and bloody tyrants as the Stuarts. Let them be done away with, in this land of liberty. Yours, in the spirit of freedom and humanity.

SOLOMON SOUTHWICK."

JAIL, Sept. 12, 1839.

Spink was cleared without trial, and Ferris acquitted. Good.

All the morning a vagrant belonging to the ball and chain gang, has been having the most horrible fits. He lies on the brick pavement, and seems to be in the most dreadful agony; rolling over and over, grinding his teeth, biting his arms and foaming at the mouth. He is covered with filthy rags and disgusting vermin.

In the forenoon I was taken to the Recorder's Court, to plead to the endictment respecting Gen. Potter. I took my seat, as I had been in the habit of doing, in the bar. I plead not guilty, to the endictment, and returned to jail. At two o'clock, I went in again to support a motion to put over the trial by an affidavit of merits. The court meantime had given an order that I should be put into the prisoner's box. So when I went out of the jail, the constable said, "Now, Mr.

Nichols, I want you to go right in and take your seat in the prisoner's box—I don't want to put you in—you just walk along and take your seat." So much more decency had the constable than the Recorder.

I went into court and spoke to a sheriff. "Mr. Stewart," said I, "have the goodness to show me a seat."

He walked along and opened the door of the prisoner's box. Every eye—bench, bar and audience—was fixed upon me.

"Mr. Stewart," said I, "which seat shall I take?"

"Just which you please," he replied; and I walked into the middle one, turned round, lay down my hat, took out a white cambrick handkerchief, dusted the seat, sat down, and taking my glass from my vest pocket, very deliberately quizzed the Recorder and Aldermen who composed the court.

The trial was put over, and I came back to my cell and wrote,

TO THE HON. H. J. S.

Dids't think, Recorder, thou coulds't me disgrace,
By giving for my seat the felon's place?
Know that I felt more honored there to be,
Than cheek-by-jole with such an ass as thee.

The plan was worthy of thy shallow wit!
And while false traitors shall beside thee sit,
Not even a felon would with thee change places,
And also change friends, characters and faces.

Thy wit is like thy *eloquence*—alas!
Not e'en Great Harry of the West could pass,
But patient stood, beneath a scorching sun,
One long, dull hour, to hear thy nonsense run.

Mean as I deem thee, I will stoop to ask
One favor—should it be thy welcome task,
Ever to sentence me, I do beseech,
Send me to jail, *but don't inflict a speech!*

JAIL, Sept. 13, 1839.

Copied two letters from the purest and dearest friend of my early days; and then I burned the originals, so long treasured; and as I held the paper in my hand, which the fire was consuming, and the words, line by line, were obliterated, I felt as if I were destroying the only memorial I possessed of the beautiful writer. I repented and would have saved it; but it was too late. I never cared for keepsakes before. Her fair hand traced those letters—she leaned over that sheet—she sighed as she wrote; perhaps tears filled her eyes. It has felt her breath. But it is folly to regret. They are safe from profanation, and the rude gaze and coarse jest of the vulgar. *I* have seen her—my hand has grasped hers—my eye has spoken to hers—my ear has drunk in the melody of her gentle voice, and once, only once, our lips were pressed together. 'Twas a moonlight summer evening, that seemed like heaven; and she, a white robed angel, stood beside me. We looked round upon the beautiful earth, and up to the blue heavens. It was a moment of such pure and holy feeling, as the earth affords but few of, in the life time of the most favored of its inhabitants. Oh! I would suffer a year's imprisonment, for one happy hour with that pure, noble and beautiful girl.

A poor, pale, crazy woman was brought to jail last night. Her madness was religious. The poor creature cried, laughed, screamed, sung and prayed. I think they beat her to make her still.

SEPTEMBER 17, 1839.

There is some hope yet. The attempt to convict Ferris and Spink of libel, has been defeated. The *clique* were boasting of their intention of sending them to jail, when, they thought, I should have to suspend the Buffalonian, and they would be relieved from the fear of further exposure.

This country never saw a conspiracy to muzzle the press, such as exists in this city. I have been fined and imprisoned as unjustly as ever man suffered; and not content with this, the infamous scoundrels wished to imprison those in my employ, and those they suspect of being in it, and if they could, would put every man in jail who dares to take my paper.

These things must have an end. If grand juries will forget their oaths, and lend themselves to do the dirty work of scoundrels; if they will endict without evidence, and upon the most frivolous and ridiculous pretexts, and refuse to find bills for high crimes and misdemeanors, where the evidence is positive and clear, there is no way but for the great body of the people to take the matter into their own hands, and right the wrongs under which the community have so long suffered.

For a time, these harpies and hypocrites may effect their object. For a time they may imprison me, derange my business, and by their stupid and malignant slanders, may prejudice the weak and the vacillating against me. They may even stop the Buffalonian, but all will not save them from destruction and infamy.

Retrospections and reflections are the order of the day.

I remember seeing once, in a fine northern city, a fat and apparently spirit soaked Recorder. He was bloated and beastly in his person, contemptible in conduct, tyrannical and arbitrary in his decisions, and to all appearance a pompous blockhead, a supple tool, and a hollow hearted knave. I do not say he was all this, but at the time, I well remember, his conduct on many occasions induced me to believe so.

This man was once comparatively popular, but in the course of a few months he became despised for his stupidity, hated for his tyranny, and for his subserviency to a noted gang of burglars, was held in general and well merited contempt.

So oppressive at last became his court, that its abolition was imperatively demanded; and covered with infamy and disgrace, he sunk back into a private station, and finally into oblivion.

I once knew of a first judge of a county in this state, who, when an officer of a temeperance society, was picked up, dead drunk, from a gutter in Albany; who one winter lay for weeks together in a state of almost continual intoxication in the lowest haunts of vice in a distant city. Who at Washington disgraced the county in which he dispenses law, by his **drunken-**

ness, loaferism and obscenity. Who has repeatedly lost all his clothes and money in houses of ill fame, and only been able to return to his residence, when furnished with money by his friends. Who has been engaged one week in trying his fellow creatures, on the bench, and the next in practising enormous and disgraceful frauds upon those whose interests were intrusted to his care. Who for the promise of a sum of money, so influenced a jury as to produce the conviction of an innocent man and then sentenced him to a cruel and unprecedented punishment.

Gen. Geo. P. Barker, one of the best lawyers, and one of the best men, that the Almighty ever made as a specimen of what he intended men should be, called to see me this morning. Seth C. Hawley, Esq., called in the afternoon. We talked upon politics, finance, morals and religion. His notions are those of a liberal, well informed man of the world; and *need I say*, agree precisely with my own? Would not the inference have been quite as strong if I had not said it? Does any one pronounce favorably of another's opinions, when they are not also his own? When you hear a man speak of another, as possessing correct notions, sound views, &c., he is paying himself no very equivocal compliment.

"Home as found." Absurd, I think in some things,

but not so very horrid. Dodge and Bragg are both gross caricatures, I am certain.

"But you know," said the juror, "you know those witnesses might have sworn to enough to convict him." This was the remark of one of the jurors on the late libel trial, to another; he was so anxious to convict that he tried to do so on what he thought a witness might have sworn to. This is Buffalo justice as managed by the clique.

SEPTEMBER 18, 1839.

Delightful visit from two ladies; one married, the other single. I was reading "Japhet in search of a Father," and thinking, every page or two, why the devil they didn't advertise in a newspaper in the *first place.* But it would have spoiled a good story.

They have got up a new temperance society, the pledge of which extends to all intoxicating drinks. These are, firstly, all distilled spirits, such as rum, gin, brandy, whiskey, &c. All, of which these form a portion, as cordials, most wines, &c. Fermented liquors, such as wine, cider, beer, porter, metheglin, &c. Lastly, extracts and tinctures of intoxicating vegetables, especially of the narcotic species. These are coffee, tea, all preparations of opium, nutmeg, and others of a less common character. Every one of these are excluded by the pledge of the new society. It is quite too general. He who imagines tea and coffee do not intoxicate, is not acquainted with the philosophy of intoxication. I know they do. I got as tipsy on strong coffee as I ever did on champaigne.

B. has been to Saratoga. He says it has been, during the summer, a very *bustling* place. One lady who wore a particular article of dress, of enormous dimensions, was seated in a public parlor, near a grandmotherly looking old lady, who observing the appearance caused by the article, asked her—

"Madam, do you expect the waters will cure you?"

"Yes, ma'am."

"Well, I guess you will have to stay a long time, for it is the *awfulest* swelling I ever saw in my life."

JAIL, SEPT. 22, 1839.

C. and F. called and talked with me about going to Texas. I don't believe in it. They hold out brilliant inducements, but I am not quite ready to leave Buffalo yet.

An hermaphrodite, the most perfect specimen I ever saw or read of, in form, features, conformation, manner and disposition, was sent to jail lately. In size, shape, gait, voice, hair, complexion, beard; in short, the whole organization, mental and physical, it is difficult to tell which sex predominates, so closely are they balanced. When dressed as a woman, she calls herself Catharine Blannerhassett, which I am assured is her real name; but when, as at present, the singular being prefers to don male habiliments, the name is Timothy Keeler. I never saw quite so extraordinary a specimen of human nature.

TUESDAY, SEPT. 24, 1839.

Wearily, Oh! But I read Gil Blas and fiddle; then I play at cards, all the games I know; all fours, cassino, loo, bragg, poker, euker, whist, faro, vingt-et-un, &c. But it is a sorry amusement. I never did like cards.

Mr. Heacock's pamphlet is out, and discloses such a scene of villanous corruption, on the part of Gen. Potter, Orlando Allen, and Judge Stryker, as should consign their names to everlasting infamy. Yet **two** of these are members of the First Presbyterian church, and the other, First Judge of Erie county!

Some of my letters from a distance, and from total strangers, are not less beautiful and sympathetic than those I receive from my friends in Buffalo. "Alice," of Albion, whom I know not, writes to me; and after alluding most feelingly to my situation, and my persecutions, she says—

"I would not, I dare not pursue this train of thought, for I but revert back again; and then—but no matter, you cannot see the trembling, warm gushing tear; nor hear the oft lisped prayer.

"Go on; still keep in the path of right, holding up the hands of Justice, nor heed the smiles of those who fawn for favor at the shrine of genius, and in its adversity turn away to blast the purity of a generous heart."

Thanks, my gentle Alice.

And Rosalie writes, "I *would* like to read your first novel. I almost wonder you have not written one. You ask me when you shall commence being an author. I say, *now*. Write, ere you have lost the glorious enthusiasm of youth. Give to the world the rich stores of intellectual wealth—the rare and beautiful gems of thought which have been bestowed upon you. Are you ambitious? Do you ever feel the 'longings after immortality?' If you do, then you must write, and your brightest dreams, your highest hopes, will be fulfilled. You *know* that this is not flattery. You know I would not stoop to flatter any one; and you know how much is within your reach. * * * *

"When you are alone and dull—when writing has become an irksome task, and books have lost their accustomed charms, then strike the harp of memory, and it will speak to you in low, sweet tones, of home and loved ones—it will tell you of boyhood's happy hours, when the future was to you a fairy scene of enchantment, and life a sweet succession of pleasures, pure and unalloyed; ere that sad lesson-giver, Experience, had taught you that you would be obliged to wrestle with malice and villany, and, I grieve to say, feel their withering effects. If by chance a wild strain should remind you of me; it will tell you of one who could she do aught to amuse and enliven the gloomy solitude which at present surrounds you, would—Oh! how gladly! Many will be louder and warmer in their professions of friendship; no friendship will stand a better test than mine."

Sweet enthusiast! the man who would not go to prison four months, and feel amply repaid by such an assurance, would be unworthy of it.

JAIL, Sept. 29, 1839.

If I leave Buffalo, I waver between New York and Texas. Pleasure calls one way, ambition the other. A. says I cannot contend successfully with this *clique*. Perhaps I cannot. Thus far they have gained but little of me. Every attempt to crush me has sunk them the deeper. A. judges of power, ambition and office, by being captain of a steamboat. Well, that is not so bad. Power is pleasant, if 'tis only to drive a span of horses.

A proposition has been made to settle the civil suits against the *clique*, stop the Buffalonian, and have me leave the city. They offer to pay seven hundred and fifty dollars, and dispose of the endictments pending against me! Fools! Do they think I will settle in that way. The offer is contemptible, and of a piece with all their conduct. Buy me off for $750. Another cypher might be considered a respectable bribe. The negociation may go on, if they wish it; but if they think I will consent to such an arrangement they are strangely mistaken.

A grave looking man in spectacles came to my door to-day, and told me I must love my Heavenly Father. I thought that was a rum go; and my first impression was that it was some insane man just committed for safe keeping; but as his vagaries are innocent he is still at large. He insisted upon the point—I must love my Heavenly Father, "whether or no;" and he was very anxious to know if I did.

When I was very young, and God the Almighty was described to me as a being merciful and good, I loved him. When I saw him portrayed in the books of Moses, as bloodthirsty, malignant, jealous and revengeful, my love and admiration cooled; and when I was taught that he had, from the beginning, destined ninety-nine hundredths of the human race to an eternity of hell torments, I rather think I began to hate him. But it was very wicked. If men want me to love my Heavenly Father, they must not make him out to be a fiend.

JAIL, Oct. 2, 1839.

Several of the sheriff's officers went to Canada last night, and kidnapped a fine looking rogue as ever graced a jail. They took him from his bed, dragged him a mile naked and barefoot, having torn off his only garment to gag him with, and then got him into a boat and brought him over. This was done without any process or pretence of authority. I blowed up the officers, called them a set of d——d piratical scoundrels—and so they are. They deserved to be shot.

Brown told me I didn't look strong enough to use such hard words; and then I damned him for starving me four months, and then twitting me of leanness. Contemptible wretch. He is fat enough, at all events.

> Monarch of misery, and fiend of fat!
> A hog his body furnished, and his soul a rat.

JAIL, Oct. 3, 1839.

SONG OF THE IMPRISONED.

> Oh! would that to-night,
> In the moonbeams so bright,
> While the earth glows with beauty, waves sparkle in light,
> I could leave this dull place,
> All my loved haunts to trace,
> Where Nature's rich beauties would burst on my sight.
>
> I'd fly to the grove,
> Once sacred to love,
> Where moonbeams, like ghosts of past pleasures, slow move;
> Or down by the lake,
> Where the still waters make
> A mirrored bright firmament, like that above,

How glorious to ride
Where the bright foaming tide
Every moment besprinkles my proud courser's side,
And the billows so white
Seem to rush on in might,
Till conquered, crest-fallen, they sullen subside.

Oh! give me the power,
For one glorious hour,
To escape from my dungeon, how wildly I'd scour
Over field, over hill,
Ever ranging at will,
Nor care though the tempests around me should lower.

Jail, Oct. 4, 1839.

TO ROSALIE.

* * * "I am not old enough, well-read enough, nor experienced enough to commence authorship. Mere enthusiasm will not answer. No one is more conscious of his own imperfections than I am. Sometimes I think I will retire, for a year or two, and study; but I have become so accustomed to business, and the world, that I fear it would be irksome. I am now in the worst of all positions, suspense. It unstrings every nerve, and renders dormant every faculty. I can neither read nor write. When I do the latter, I am conscious of its stupidity, and so it must be for ten days to come; but it seems as if that the moment I step out of this detestable place, I shall feel a new life and energy springing up within me, for some purpose, as yet unknown. * * *

"I have just witnessed a scene of human suffering, but I cannot write it out. It was too terrible, and sickens me to think of. That poor creature struggling and raving so horribly, with fixed, staring eyes, biting her flesh, gnashing her teeth in agony, while the foam flew from her lips, and it took four stout men to hold her. And now the poor, wretched creature is moaning of her home, and her mother, and the cruelty which drove her to punishment and crime. Poor creature! And she has known love, friendship, and maternal affection, and home and happiness. Now she is kept in this foul den of torture. Did our Father in Heaven make his creatures for scenes and sufferings like these?"

As the day of Freedom approaches, I write less, and still less. I think of the future, and a thousand plans present themselves for my adoption. At one time I am ho! for Texas! and ambition. At another

I sigh for a life of literary ease and social pleasure, and my thoughts turn to the Commercial Emporium; and then I feel determined to stay in Buffalo and see the end of this coil. Circumstances must direct me. If my friends wish it, and are willing to take hold as I have a right to expect they will, I am with them.

Monday, Oct. 7, 1839.

My benefit comes off at the theatre on Wednesday evening. The object is ostensibly to pay my fine. The prospect is an excitement of no ordinary character. Mr. and Mrs. Lewis have volunteered, also Frank Johnson & Co., of Philadelphia. There is a prospect of a splendid house. Will the clique like that? The bills and tickets have pictures of prison grates upon them, and the affair is pushed on with true Buffalonian enthusiasm.

Letters—letters from home, East, and from my charming correspondents here, who are very kind to write to me so often.

JAIL, Thursday, Oct. 10, 1839.

The benefit came off gloriously. Such a house was never seen in Buffalo. It was crammed from pit to gallery; hundreds filled the lobbies and stair cases, and still hundreds who had bought tickets, went away without gaining admission. People came twenty miles from the country and from Canada, to attend.

There had been no committee, no drumming up the recruits. It was a demonstration of public sentiment of which I have a right to feel proud, and for which I do feel grateful.

The first piece was the Hypocrite, played admirably, by Mrs. Pierce, Mr. Dean, Mr. Wills, and company. Mrs. Lewis appeared in the French Spy.

Mrs. Pierce, in her happiest manner, recited the following address, written for the occasion:

ADDRESS.

Ye friends of Freedom! in her sacred cause,
And in defence of violated laws,
The Drama here, on her untrammelled stage,
Censures the vice and folly of the age.
'Twas thus in Greece, when first fair Freedom smiled;
And while the hours she sportively beguiled,

Each tyrant trembled in his secret lair,
Lest he should see himself depicted there!
'Twas ever thus—so ever may it be;
The Drama's temple, home of Liberty!
Ye never can be slaves, while ye possess
A stage uncensored, and an unbribed press;
Thanks to your patriot sires, ye have them still,
And here's the promise that ye ever will.

But Ah! amid the splendors of this night,
Another scene now opens on my sight;
Dark, massive walls, and iron grates, in gloom
Surround the lonely captive's living tomb.
Not his the festive scene of revelry;
He shuts his loathing eyes on agony!
Not his the music of celestial strains;
But creaking doors and ever-clanking chains,
The maniac's shriek, the sick man's midnight moan,
The convict's bitter curse, Despair's deep groan.
Not his the happy home and fireside joys,
Where converse sweet each social hour employs;
But days and weeks and months slow creep along,
And each dull hour swells the dark heap of wrong.
Still in the firmness of unconquered truth,
Full of the glowing hopes of buoyant youth,
The captive braves his tyrants' purchased power,
And patient waits for the avenging hour.
When shall the hour arrive, when that vile clique
Shall taste the vengeance they on others wreak?
How long shall worth before corruption quail,
And honor, justice, truth be buried in a jail?

I read the answer in your flashing eyes.
Now let a brighter scene before you rise.
When Fraud and Crime shall shrink abashed away,
And honest Merit bask in Fortune's ray;
When Truth shall triumph over treacherous arts,
Nor Justice seek in vain, from generous hearts;
And he, to be Truth's champion, who will dare,
Shall win the approving smiles of all the brave and fair.

Enthusiastic applause greeted every sentence. A Comic Song, by Mr. Lewis, an original Fireman's Song, by Mr. Rice, and the music of Frank Johnson's band, were also among the evening's entertainments. The only regret was, that the theatre, for one night, could not have been swelled to ten times its capacity.

When the performances were over, nine cheers for Nichols were given in the street, and in a few moments the jail yard was filled. I was cheered again, and was obliged to do what I hate, make a speech through the gratings, to thank them. It was short, and sweet, judging by the hurras that followed it. Then I went back to my cell, and supped on Champaigne and oysters, smuggled in for the occasion. The receipts were over one thousand dollars—more, by almost one half, than those of any benefit ever given in Buffalo. So emphatically has been expressed,

THE PEOPLE'S VERDICT

Jail, Oct. 11, 1839.

This has been one of the longest days yet; cold and blue-devilish. W. & B. called and told me of a stupid slander in circulation, of my extorting twenty-five dollars for suppressing some scandal. What humbug! I might have taken thousands. Again and again I have had opportunities to make my own terms, but I defy any man to bring an instance where I have taken one cent. Knaves will of course believe such stories. They judge me by themselves.

When I sat down, I thought I could write on, interminably; but writing, for the love of it, I cannot do. I can write letters, editorials, any thing, when I have an object, but not a journal, for no eye but my own. Why should I? "I hae nae motive."

Jail, Tuesday, Oct. 15, 1839..

One day more, and Liberty!
John Low is confined in jail, after living for three weeks in the city and suburbs, in defiance of the whole police. He is not allowed to talk with me, but

has sent me the following account of the attempt to Morganize me, which is worthy of the characters of those engaged in it. He calls his account the

SECRETS OF THE CELLAR.

It was eight oclock, and but few of the conspirators had assembled. "They will be here soon," says D.; "and by J——s C——st! you will see some of the greatest men here, that's in the city—Old Slade, and Wilgus, *and* Buckland; and, by J——s C——st! I can't tell you all; but, by J——s C——st! we'll have that office torn to h–ll before we sleep, by J——s C——st! Noyes will go his length, and they will back us through thick and thin, by J——s C——st!"

Now the company had mostly assembled, and we proceeded to business. "Well," said Hank; "have you got corks, boys?—if you aint, I have; and by J——s C——st! black yourselves good." So at it we went, blacking ourselves, and dressing to suit the occasion; some with old caps, some with red shirts, and old clothes, procured for that purpose.

When we had got ready, Hank looked amazed. He did not know us, and exclaimed, with his hands lifted up about as high as he could reach—"Well, by

J——s C——st! Well, by G–d! nobody would know you, by J——s C——st! Just look at them," said Hank, and they all took a regular grin, old and young. Then the old chaps left.

"Now," says little Charley, "we must have some liquor." A bottle was procured, and then there was some trouble to raise the funds. B. had none, and S. none, and two or three more had none; and here they begun to back out; but some one raised a quarter, and another a half, and all went on smoothly again. When that was gone it had got so late that the shops were shut, and we could get no more of the creature.

It was nearly twelve, and time to proceed to business. "Now, by J——s C——st!" said Hank, "we must have two parties; one to take Nichols and tar and feather him, and the other to go to the office and demolish that. And by J——s C——st! we must have Mount's wagon to carry Nichols off out of the city, to do the business;" and off Hank sent one of the number to procure it.

"Now," continued Hank, getting upon the table, "by J——s C——st! I am authorized to give you twenty-five dollars each, and if my word of honor is worth any thing, by J——s C——st! you shall have it."

The parties started for their posts. One was to watch for Nichols, while the other remained in the cellar until he was caught, and then repair immediately to the office. The first party met with a failure, so we all started for the office; but before we got there, some of the most anxious fell behind, and some have never been seen since. When we got back to the cellar, we found Hank crouching in one corner, as if afraid of the leather-heads; and now there was another small failure. Instead of twenty-five dollars each, we got only ten; deducting fifteen for not taking Nichols. "Well, by J——s C——st!" said Hank, "that's a bad move, by G–d!"

Such is a description of this affair, by one of the actors, in which was engaged that clique of villany, who, for two years have been trying to destroy me, and through whose influence I have suffered four months of close, unjust imprisonment and brutal tyranny; now at an end, for to-morrow I shall be once more a free man.

END OF THE JOURNAL.

APPENDIX.

Thus my Journal. I have copied the foregoing pages, almost *verbatim et literatim*, from four MS. volumes. The correspondence I found too voluminous to give entire. Some I have left out altogether.

On my first day of Freedom, I went into court and entered bail on the three remaining endictments. At two o'clock, a committee of the citizens of Hamburgh visited me at the jail, with a congratulatory address. Main-street was full; ladies had collected at the windows—some had even prepared wreaths to crown my freedom. A sumptuous collation was laid at the Mansion House, and thousands assembled to see me. I disappointed them all. Never did I feel less inclined for a public show. I was grateful to the people for their feelings, but I wished to pass the first hour of liberty more alone. A carriage drove to the gate, and amid the hurras of hundreds of my friends,

I drove off, out of town, into the old forests, where I could breathe the air of freedom amid the sublimities of nature. Oh! the ecstacy of that hour!

When I returned towards the city I was met with carriages and banners, a band of music, and demonstrations of popular feeling. There could not be a warmer welcome to Liberty.

Not content with being at large, talking with my friends, and enjoying the blessings of social intercourse, I took a steamboat trip to Cleveland. I was in an ecstacy of enjoyment. Strangers must have thought me mad. I returned, and made preparations to enlarge the Buffalonian. The stock certificates of the "Buffalonian Free Press Association," with a capital of ten thousand dollars, were lithographed, and a considerable portion of the stock subscribed for; when, at a blow, all my prospects were destroyed. The clique, disappointed in the effect of my imprisonment, finding me too firm to be bought or frightened, resorted to the basest stratagem. They got in their power, private manuscripts, which might seriously affect my friends, and pretended information, which, though false, was none the less injurious to those I felt bound to protect. By these means they coerced me into a settlement, on their own terms. I had but one *honorable* course to take—those who know me, need not be assured that I did not hesitate to adopt it. Upon payment of a certain sum of money, I released them from a civil action for damages in the destruction of the Buffalonian office, and in consideration of their giving up all the papers and memoranda in their possession, and causing *nolle prosequi* to be entered upon the endictments against me, the publication of the Buffalonian was suspended. Then the game of iniquity went on unchecked. The accounts of Rathbun were sold by the assignees and bid in by a gang of sharpers, who made use of the grossest bribery and corruption, to enrich themselves and defraud the creditors of the estate. Hiram Pratt, one of the assignees, paid to one man a thousand dollars, to prevent competition on three notes, and cheated the creditors out of $7,500 by the operation. This is only one instance. The matter is before the Chancellor, and it is to be hoped will be properly investigated.

B. Rathbun is in a State Prison—Hiram Pratt is furnishing a splendid marble palace with the most costly and luxurious furniture, while widows and orphans are suffering by the dishonest assignee, the ingrate, and the traitor.

Will the clique, of which he has been the right hand in all villany, be sustained in their influence at home and abroad? So long as the vilest corruption

APPENDIX.

can do it, they will. While, as at the last election, open bribery, and official coercion is used by the highest officers of the city, and the people wink at, or justify, such enormities, Buffalo must feel their blasting influence.

Gentle reader! I cannot fancy the impression these pages may have made upon you; nor am I very anxious. Momentary influence has governed me, and often, circumstances of which you, I earnestly hope, may never be able to judge. There are, doubtless, some foolish things; for I am a devout believer in the utility of nonsense. I suppose there are some clever things—for the world has given me credit for ability to write them. There are some sentimental things, especially in my prison cosrrespondence; and for copying which, I suppose I shall get well pouted at. There are egotistical things, of necessity; and would have been, whether it were necessary or not. But, on the whole, how do you like it?

FINIS.